All Gardens Great & Small

REBECCA POW

Photographs by Caroline Shipsey

HALSGROVE
in association with
HTV WEST

First published in 1998 by Halsgrove Books
Copyright © 1998 HTV West

ISBN 1 84114 001 5

British Library Cataloguing-in-Publication-Data
A CIP data for this book is available from the British Library

HALSGROVE
Halsgrove House
Lower Moor Way
Tiverton EX16 6SS
T: 01884 243242
F: 01884 243325
www.halsgrove.com

Printed and bound in Italy
by Editoriale Libraria, Trieste

CONTENTS

FOREWORD

For many years I have been involved in making and presenting gardening and related programmes for HTV and Channel 4. It had always struck me that there was a series to be done simply on the beauty of many of the outstanding gardens within the West Country alone. The idea was not to make a practical gardening programme about, for example, how to take geranium cuttings, but to concentrate on the artistic nature of the gardens themselves and to delve into the minds of the clever people who have created them.

I wanted the programmes, and the book produced in conjunction with them, to be attractive not only to those who garden themselves but to anyone who appreciates lovely things and enjoys visiting works of art. That is how I believe many of the living masterpieces created by the gardeners featured should be regarded.

There seem to be common threads among all those featured in the book, whether they be owners or head gardeners: they have a passion for their gardens, and an awareness that what they are doing is beautiful, therapeutic, and can perhaps be shared by others and preserved for the nation, in however small a way, for the future.

Often gardening programmes overlook the winter months of the year, so in the *All Gardens Great and Small* series we were determined to cover every season. I think you will find that some of the gardens featured look just as captivating in the winter and early spring as others do in the summer and autumn.

In writing a book to accompany the series, the idea was to produce not just a coffee-table book but one that would act as a useful guide to all the gardens. So this book gives details such as location and opening times, facilities, and what to expect when you arrive. In addition there is a tour of each garden which points out the main attractions, and its history where appropriate. Of course, a fascinating insight is also given into the people behind the gardens themselves, revealing what inspires and drives them. Planting suggestions are provided for each garden, so that, should you decide to put into practice any design ideas that appeal to you, you will have a point of reference from which to start.

Meeting all of the gardeners featured was an inspiration. We had to film come rain or shine (and once snow), so for many of them it was often a chilly and lengthy process.

Following in our wake came the trusty stills photographer, Caroline Shipsey. Aided by her many years of experience, she has managed to capture the essence of what each of the gardens is about.

I hope you enjoy the book. It was certainly a pleasure writing it, even if it did make me want to get out and completely revamp my entire garden!

Rebecca Pow, 1998

ACKNOWLEDGEMENTS

I should like to thank all the participants in the series who so willingly opened up their gardens for us to film and photograph. A thank you also to Mary Payne, Sue Rugg and Charles Clark for all their help. And I must particularly thank HTV for supporting the idea of the series and for giving me the opportunity to write the accompanying book. In addition the series would also not have been possible without the commitment of the crew: Mike Hastie, Mike Lomas, Tony Griggs and Paddy McMullin.

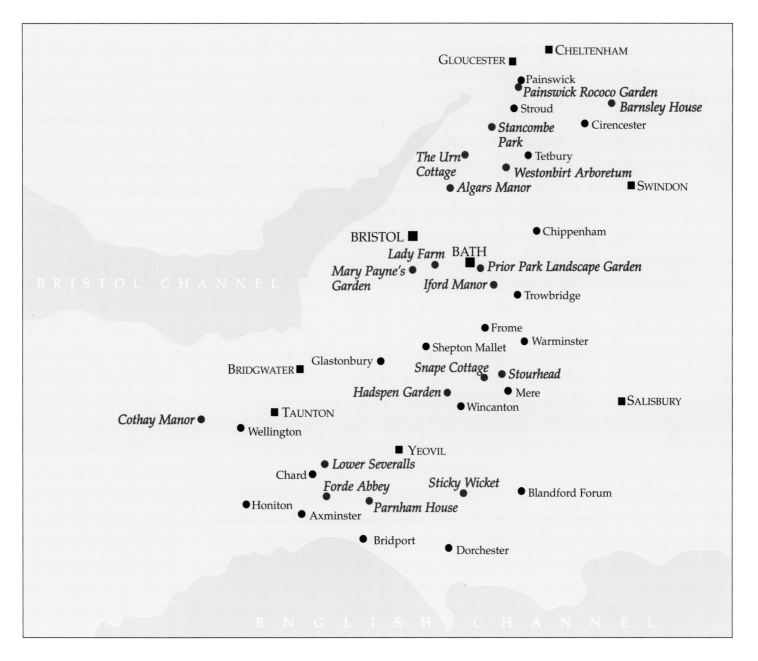

■ CHELTENHAM
GLOUCESTER ■
● Painswick
● *Painswick Rococo Garden*
● Stroud   ● *Barnsley House*
● *Stancombe*   ● Cirencester
Park
The Urn ●   ● Tetbury
Cottage   ● *Westonbirt Arboretum*
● *Algars Manor*   ■ SWINDON

● Chippenham

BRISTOL ■   BATH
● *Lady Farm*   ■
Mary Payne's   ● *Prior Park Landscape Garden*
Garden   ● *Iford Manor* ●
                    ● Trowbridge

● Frome
● Warminster
● Shepton Mallet
BRIDGWATER ■   Glastonbury ●   *Snape Cottage*
                    ● *Stourhead*
Hadspen Garden ●   ● Mere
                    ● Wincanton   ■ SALISBURY

Cothay Manor ●   ■ TAUNTON
● Wellington

■ YEOVIL
● *Lower Severalls*
Chard ●
● *Forde Abbey*   *Sticky Wicket*
● Honiton   ● *Parnham House* ●   ● Blandford Forum
● Axminster

● Bridport   ● Dorchester

BRISTOL CHANNEL

ENGLISH CHANNEL

7

SPRING GARDENS

BARNSLEY HOUSE

Rosemary and Charles Verey

Barnsley, Cirencester, Gloucestershire GL7 5EE
Tel. 01285 740281 and 01285 740561

LOCATION
In the village of Barnsley, 4 miles (6.5 km) north-east of Cirencester on the B4425.

VISITING
Open Mon., Wed., Thurs. and Sat., 10am–6pm.
Admission: £3.50 adults, £2.50 OAPs, children free.
(No charge in December and January.) Parties by appointment only.

FACILITIES
Nursery selling unusual plants.

KEY FEATURES
Mature garden with interesting collection of shrubs and trees
Herbaceous borders
Laburnum walk
Knot and herb gardens
Decorative potager
Gothic summerhouse
Temple garden

*Anybody who walks in this garden must realize that I'm very
keen on knots and patterns and using box edging and clipped
things. I also believe it's most important to have an exuberance of
planting and at the same time a very strong structure.*

(Rosemary Verey)

The garden at Barnsley House is an all-year-round garden, but in springtime the burgeoning beds of herbaceous plants, set off by the artfully trained and clipped bushes and trees, make it a place definitely worth visiting at this time of year.

And garden visiting is something Rosemary, even with all her expertise in garden design, highly recommends:

'It's terribly important when you're keen on gardening to go and visit other people's gardens and to read books. And when you see a brilliant idea put it in the back of your mind or write it down, and then one day you may be able to copy that idea yourself.'

Rosemary also openly admits that she's been keen to encourage the advice of friends regarding her own garden. She claims that many of the philosophies she now holds have been moulded by a whole collection of well-known names in the gardening and design world, such as Sir Roy Strong and Christopher Lloyd.

Barnsley House

The garden itself is enclosed by a high stone wall built in 1770, a hundred years later than the handsome Cotswold-stone house. The garden, as seen today, has evolved since 1960. Together with her husband, David, an architectural historian, Rosemary has aimed to develop a country garden with formal and historical features but overflowing with plants and interest all year.

Since there are no views out of the garden it has been imperative to create vistas within it. At every turn therefore there is a new experience and something else to discover.

In Front of the House

Before you reach the garden, your appetite is whetted by a walk through the nursery, which is brim-full of tempting plants. Then, as you step through an arched doorway the broad expanse of Barnsley House Garden opens up before you. Down the centre of the front lawns runs a crazy-paving path lined on either side by neatly clipped yews. The path looks very natural, with plants bursting out from between the stones.

The lawns are surrounded by a range of parterre beds which are fine examples of the exuberance of planting Rosemary so loves. In springtime the tulips are much in evidence. In the bed outside the shop 'White Triumphator' and 'Yellow Dover' predominate, along with the unusual, orange streaked with purple, *Tulipa* 'Prinses Irene.'

In the parallel bed the spring bulb colours are kept to white, cream and pink with bursts of purple. And in the bed beside the garden gate hellebores are still proving good value, the paeony leaves are emerging and narcissus and tulips are appearing through a delicate carpet of forget-me-nots.

Beside this bed is a herb garden, prettily created out of a pattern of diamond-shaped box hedges. Straight away Rosemary's leaning towards patterns in the garden is evident.

Box hedging has been used to create a patterned herb bed.

beyond. If you had a small garden you could make that a central feature all by itself. And I love the hollies, *Ilex altaclarensis* 'Golden King'. I call them my old men. We have to clip them every year. It's rather like going to the hairdresser's – if you didn't your hair would get untidy and the hollies would too.'

ROSEMARY'S FAVOURITE PLANTS FOR STRUCTURE

Hebe rakaiensis	Maintains its own perfect dome shape
Ilex x *altaclarensis* 'Golden King'	Variegated holly; clip to shape
Juniperus communis 'Hibernica'	Irish juniper; 14-foot (4-metre) columns
Buxus sempervirens 'Suffruticosa'	Dwarf box; for edging and creating patterns
Salix daphnoides 'Aglaia'	Pale purple catkins open in February

ROSEMARY'S FAVOURITE 'EXUBERANT BORDER' PLANTS

Rheum palmatum rubrum	Stately rhubarb plant; large umbrella-like, palm-shaped leaves, claret red undersides
Tulipa 'China Pink'	Pale pink lily-flowered tulips; harmonize well with Rheum
Tulipa 'Prinses Irene'	Orange tulips streaked with purple; effective planted with cowslips (*Primula veris*)
Myosotis	Forget-me-not; ideal for under-planting
Narcissus 'Thalia'	White, double-headed, sweetly scented

Even from here the strong structure is obvious, in particular the use of horizontal and vertical lines to draw the eye.

'You've got to have contrast and things that are also in harmony with each other,' she explains. 'Take these fifteen-year-old Irish junipers, for example. They make a marvellous statement with the standard euonymous and standard privet

*The temple was brought to Barnsley House
from Fairford Park, Gloucestershire.*

The Frog Fountain and Border

Passing the Gothick summerhouse, which forms a focal point from the side of the house and catches the light beautifully as the sun goes down in the evening, you wander through an inviting archway, moving from shade into a light-filled path with borders on each side. The splashing water of the Frog Fountain (carved by Simon Verity) attracts immediate attention. It is surrounded by *Ligularia dentata* 'Desdemona' and *L. przewalskii*, with a sprinkling of narcissus and white and dark-red tulips in spring.

From the fountain area three parallel paths radiate out, each with a different feel and vista. A broad grass pathway leads down the centre, ultimately to the Temple Garden. In spring, here too a profusion of tulips predominate in the wide beds to either side of of the path, themed in blocks of pale yellow and white. The second path, paved with pebbles collected by the Vereys from the beach years ago, runs under an arch of laburnum with wisterias twining through it.

'I have under-planted with red tulips, which flower in April and May,' Rosemary tells us. 'They are in a sea of forget-me-nots, and since I like the ground to be covered all year, these will be followed by *Allium hollandicum* in June and hostas from July until September.'

From the laburnum arch you stay under leafy cover, passing straight to a long tunnel of pleached limes (*Tilia platyphyllos* 'Rubra'), an idea started by David Verey in 1959.

The third path from the fountain is the Winter Walk, lined with box balls that stand out in winter, especially on frosty mornings.

The Temple Garden

This is dominated by a grand Tuscan temple. 'It loves being here!' laughs Rosemary. 'It's the same date as the garden wall and was originally built in Fairford Park, but on falling into disrepair was given to my husband, who brought it here, stone by stone, and rebuilt it. And it fits in a treat!'

The pool has since been designed around the temple. The planting is simple but effective and reflections are used to their best advantage.

'This fits into my whole philosophy,' Rosemary explains. 'I don't like the idea of garden rooms. I like to have different areas, but not separated. Here you've got the Temple Garden, but you can see the rest of the garden through the wrought-iron fencing.'

The Potager

Away from the walled garden and across a bumpy lane is the vegetable patch that is Rosemary's pride and joy. Her obsession with patterns shines through unmistakeably here, for the Potager is as decorative as it is productive. The inspiration came from sixteenth- and seventeenth-century gardening books.

The paths create the patterns, carefully laid out using old bricks, and each bed is edged with varieties of box, alpine strawberries, lavender and chives. Box pyramids and balls mark the corners of some beds. And in every bed is a different crop, planned in strict rotation: peas and beans followed by brassicas and then root vegetables. Is it labour-intensive?

'Truthfully, it is less work than a conventional vegetable area,' answers Rosemary, 'because the ground is divided into small areas, which means when you're planting seed or harvesting you don't have to tread on the ground. There's very little digging, and the box hedging protects the young plants.'

The whole area is very much an artist's palette. Lettuce varieties are chosen not just for their taste, but for the colour of their leaves or the texture of their foliage. Fruit trees are trained in an array of fascinating patterns. And between everything burst out bright flowers, to attract the insects as well as for artistic effect. In the spring one of Rosemary's favourite combinations is the planting of lettuces and parsley among tulips.

Even though Rosemary Verey is heading for her eightieth year, her enthusiasm and sparkle seem undiminished. At every turn as she wanders her garden she has an eye open for anything out of place, such as a stray weed or a plant in need of attention. And the bevy of trainee gardeners

The Potager

Rosemary takes under her wing are kept well in check. She is still constantly dashing off across the world to lecture, advise on and design gardens, but she remains very much in charge back at Barnsley.

'People often ask me what's going to happen to this garden eventually,' she says. 'I really honestly haven't formulated my idea of what I want the garden to be in ten or twenty years' time. I just hope that someone goes on loving it.'

ALGARS MANOR

(Private garden)

Dr John Naish and Dr Barbara Naish

Iron Acton, Bristol BS37 9TB

Tel. 01454 228372

LOCATION

Algars Manor is in Iron Acton, 9 miles (14.5 km) north of Bristol and
3 miles (5 km) West of Yate. Turn south off the Iron Acton bypass (B4059).
Pass the village green, continue 200 yards/metres and bear left over the
level crossing (Station Road). Algars is on the left.

VISITING

As detailed in *Gardens of England and Wales Open For Charity* ('The Yellow
Book'). Usually open on dates in March and April, including Easter Sunday.

FACILITIES

Teas in the garden on open days. Guided tours by
appointment. Picnic areas.

KEY FEATURES

3-acre (1.2-hectare) woodland garden beside River Frome
Mill stream
Camellias, magnolias, daffodils, and azaleas
Exotic and native trees

*I really love magnolias. They're about the oldest flowering plant,
dating from 50 million years ago. They're extremely beautiful during their
flowering period and quite a few are beautiful in winter with lovely silvery
buds. I just thought it would be a dream to make this a home for magnolias.
It had previously been an untouched English woodland, full of brambles,
nettles and every horror you could think of.*

(John Naish)

For forty-five years Dr Naish has laboured to create his ideal garden. Inspired by a visit to Caerhays Castle in Cornwall in 1953, he determined to develop a similar garden on a small scale. He obtained just the location when he bought Algars Manor, which came complete with a section of valley through which rushed the River Frome.

It was an arduous task for many years, since the valley was densely wooded and overgrown. Having a demanding schedule as a consultant at the nearby Frenchay Hospital, John was able to carry out his clearance work only at weekends. And early on, few of the rhododendrons and other plants he added to the woodland flourished. This was largely because the elm trees that predominated in the area were taking away most of the nutrients and water from the soil. It was an accident of nature that gave John his first big helping hand, as he explains:

'When Dutch elm disease came along in 1970 it was a

Algars Manor is at its best in springtime, when the magnolias are in full bloom.

blessing in disguise, because when the elms went, it enabled more light to get in and more water and nutrients became available. And at last some of my plantings of camellias and magnolias started to take off.'

From those early days the valley has grown into a natural-style woodland garden where a mixture of native and exotic plant and tree species grow cheek by jowl. The garden is open in the spring because this is when it is at its peak. Daffodils drift down the steep slopes, poking up through the periwinkle that acts as ground cover, and everywhere the brilliant blossoms of the magnolia trees and the flourescent pinks of the camellias create the impression of some far-off foreign land.

The Magnolia Walk

John has over fifty magnolias in the garden from over thirty-eight different varieties, and despite his eighty-three years is still eagerly on the lookout for new specimens that take his fancy. He's particularly excited by the great surge in breeding that has occurred recently through hybridization.

'Now there are five times as many varieties as there were when I started here in the 1950s,' he says, 'and this enables you to buy hybrids which are guaranteed to flower on average three to four years after putting them in, which is years quicker than with the traditional varieties. It's like being a surfer riding the crest of a wave; it is breaking all around you and you're enjoying it!'

One such example of a new hybrid can be seen at the top of the Magnolia Walk: *Magnolia* x 'Heaven Scent'. It was bred in America by Dr Todd Gresham, one of the great authorities on hybrids. John's specimen has been in the ground for fifteen years, and flowered after just five. The tree is now bigger than some John planted over forty years ago, and

Magnolia x loebneri 'Merrill' forms a magnificent backdrop to the Japanese bridge.

garden, forty-five years ago. It is not a hybrid and it still hasn't flowered! This shows how truly devoted a grower must be to plant something knowing how long the wait may be until it can be seen in its full glory.

The water running through the garden provides a splendid mirror for the magnolias, many of whose branches droop down to the water's edge. The image of the glistening white *Magnolia x loebneri* 'Merrill' that forms a backdrop beyond the arching Japanese bridge at the far end of the garden is unforgettable.

Always keen to encourage others to try his beloved magnolias, John has some valuable advice on which ones to begin with and how to care for them:

'In a small suburban garden new hybrids, like those nicknamed 'The Washington Girls', are ideal. They have the great virtue of flowering a bit later than other varieties and so don't often get damaged by frost. They can tolerate a bit of lime in the soil and won't grow too large. Remember to be sure never to knock the tree with the lawnmower and never to fork round it, because they have very superficial roots. If you give it a good chance and water it in the first year it should look after itself and be a pleasure for years and years to come.'

JOHN'S FAVOURITE MAGNOLIAS

Magnolia x 'Susan'/'Jane'/'Ricki'/'Pinkie' ('The Washington Girls')	Hybrids, suitable for small gardens; various colours, from red to deep fuschia; lily-shaped flowers late into May
Magnolia x *loebneri* 'Leonard Messel'	Small hybrid with pale pink star-shaped

looks very graceful with its pure pink flowers casting reflections in the mill stream below.

Right beside it, as if in testimony to the success of the new hybrids, stands one of the very first magnolias planted in the

	petals from March to end April
Magnolia x 'Heaven Scent'	Medium-sized, fast-flowering hybrid; pure pink, vase-shaped flowers
Magnolia x *loebneri* 'Merrill'	Large tree; white flowers out before the leaves; won an RHS award of garden merit

Camellias

John's other love is camellias, a group of plants in which is included the tea plant. In March and April the brilliant pink hues of many camellias adorn the garden. Venture into the small old worked-out quarry (the Pennant sandstone it produced having been used to build the house), and in this sheltered spot you'll see a magnificent *Camellia reticulata* x 'Francie L', with flowers as big as saucers. John is also proud of another tender plant that is flourishing here, an *Acacia dealbata* (Mimosa) whose soft, fluffy yellow flowers are a treat to see on a chilly spring day.

As John says, 'It is very pleasing to have succeeded where many people fail to get an acacia to live through the winter and then to flower.'

He has a leaning towards plants that are a challenge to grow, and elsewhere in the garden there are unusual trees or plants, including various varieties of pieris and a collection of trees in the Barbaraetum (named after John's wife Barbara). These include a tulip tree, a rare pine from Arizona, a fern-leaf beech and a collection of rare Sorbus. Long years of treating sick human beings seem to have given John the knack of cultivating healthy plants.

'I've been involved in medicine all my life and there is an enormous similarity between the care of plants and the care of humans,' he agrees. 'It's true you're dealing with sick human beings but if you're a good doctor you should also be interested in keeping people healthy and that's what you have to do with plants. You have to give them light, you must feed them no more and no less than they need, and give them water. Yes, the similarities are tremendous, and that's why you often find a doctor's main hobby is gardening.'

John and his wife make an excellent team. The garden is a great delight to them and even at eighty-three John still spends at least two hours working there a day, although now Barbara does a lot of the heavier work such as lawnmowing and pruning. The two of them are continually planning, scheming and perfecting their woodland dream. For John there is no question of stopping:

Dr John Naish

'The future at my age is bound to be uncertain, but Barbara and I have decided to go on behaving as if the future is unlimited, and if we find something new we would like in our garden we go out and buy it and plant it. I look forward to the future – even though it may mean the end of me – quite happily, because I feel I've left something behind in this garden which will live on.'

FORDE ABBEY

Mark and Lisa Roper

Chard, Somerset TA2O 4LU. Tel. 01460 221290

LOCATION
Pick up signs for Forde Abbey in Chard, either on the A358 Chard to Axminster road, or the A30 between Chard and Crewkerne.

VISITING
Gardens open daily throughout the year, 10am–4.30pm. Abbey open 1pm–4.30pm, Sun., Wed., Easter and Bank Holidays, 1 April–end October. Coaches and private tours of the Abbey by arrangement. Admission to house and gardens: adults £5, OAPs £4.75, children free. Garden only: adults £3.75, OAPs £3.50, children free.

FACILITIES
Shop, tearoom, parking. Abbey Nursery, selling rare and unusual plants and shrubs. 'Pick your own fruit', June–August.

KEY FEATURES
Cistercian monastery set in 30-acre (12-hectare) gardens with four lakes
Temple
Crocuses in February/March
Rock garden with cyclamen
Specimen trees
Bog garden, herbaceous border and walled vegetable garden
(best from May onwards)

The garden is open every day of the year. It really is great fun apart from being economically essential. We meet an enormous number of very interested and appreciative people. I honestly do think that when a garden is cultivated like this for just one family it has missed a dimension. I think it must be shared.

(Mark Roper)

Forde Abbey, a twelfth-century
Cistercian monastery

Afeeling of peace and tranquillity emanates from Forde Abbey. Many say this stems from the days when the place was one of the great monasteries of the South West. For 400 years the Cistercian monks held sway here until in 1539 Henry VIII ordered the dissolution of the monasteries. The Abbey was turned into a house when it fell into private hands in the seventeenth century. After many changes of ownership, the property and lands came to the Roper family four generations ago.

Much of the layout of the garden seen today was created in the 1700s by the Gwyn family. The series of lakes, with their three waterfalls one above the other, date from this time. They were fashioned from the pools previously used by the monks to generate power.

Over the years the Roper family have left their mark too, creating a garden that is always changing through the seasons, as Mark enthuses:

'The garden covers thirty acres and one could garden it with difficulty, but it is divided into sections, which helps. The herbaceous borders are a relatively small part of it, but there's something to see in every season, whether it be bulbs in the spring, wild flowers, the bog garden with its primulas in May or the borders all summer.'

The Crocuses

If you want to be absolutely bowled over by a floral spectacle, the time to come to Forde Abbey is definitely late February to early March. Then the carpet of purple crocuses that stretches right across the vast lawns is unbelievable! Timing is of the essence, though (as we discovered when trying to arrange filming), because crocuses open only when the sun shines and the impact is not the same if they are tightly shut.

A spectacular carpet of Crocus vernus *and* Crocus tommasinianus *stretches across the lawn, intermixed with narcissus.*

The crocuses were originally planted by Mark's grandmother. They are mainly of two varieties: *Crocus vernus*, the truly wild crocus that forms massive purple drifts, and *Crocus tommasinianus*, which has smaller flowers on longer stems, in paler purple drifts. The crocuses have spread and thrived partly because they love the gravelly soil on the site, but especially because of the careful management they have received, as Mark explains:

'They will spread wherever you don't cut the grass until mid-summer. They do this via bulbs underground and by seed. The seedpods appear in mid June and it is essential to give them time to burst and spread.'

The Rock Garden

Tucked away at the top of the front lawn is the large Rock Garden. It was created just before the First World War out of an old gravel pit. Here you are likely to find Mark's sister, Charlotte, beavering away tending the alpine plants.

Charlotte has been largely responsible for the restoration of this area, which had become sadly choked with weeds. She was inspired and helped by Jack Drake, an alpine plantsman who, until he retired to nearby Crewkerne, ran the well-known Inshriach nursery in Scotland.

Cyclamen coum *is the star of the Rock Garden*

'It has been hard, but quite fun,' Charlotte tells us. 'You have to think big when planting up such a large rockery. The key to keeping it healthy is to top-dress the whole thing once or twice a year to make the ground between the rocks really friable.'

In the late winter and early spring time the real show-stopper in the Rock Garden is the bank of *Cyclamen coum*. In every shade from brilliant pink to clear white, the flowers cascade over the rocks in a torrent. Here and there the star-shaped blue faces of *Chionodoxa luciliae* peep through to complete the picture. Charlotte is justly proud of the results she has achieved here:

'Just over a decade ago there were only a few cyclamen in evidence. Year by year I took the weeds off the bank and with the help of leaf mould in the summer they've gradually come back. They were originally planted by my grandmother, and the corms are still in the ground. They go on growing each year and now are very big and very deep. These plants have got their corms down so far between the rocks, they can still get plenty of moisture.'

CHARLOTTE'S FAVOURITES FOR ROCKERIES IN FEBRUARY

Cyclamen coum	Shades from bright pink to white; flowers December–March
Chionodoxa luciliae	Gentian blue, star-shaped flowers; likes shade
Hepatica nobilis	Pure white flowers, early spring; likes shade
Erica carnea 'Myretoun Ruby'	Deep, soft, red; dramatic spot plant

Primula sibthorpii

Pale lilac pink dwarf; free-flower ing; responds to splitting

The Trees

There are some majestic tree specimens dotted across the garden that won't fail to attract attention. The tallest single-leaved ash in the country stands beside the Great Pond and nearby two massive redwoods, a coastal redwood, and a sierra redwood. Both were planted in the middle of the last century and are now huge.

However, probably the most dramatic-looking tree is the great column of the incense cedar (*Calocedrus decurrens*) that stretches skyward like Cleopatra's Needle. Regarded as one of the finest specimens in the country, it is located on the Mount, a raised area created in the early eighteenth century to give views down over the house and lake. Here there is one more brilliantly coloured plant to see: the *Cornus mas* 'Elegantissima', whose bright yellow flowers shower the tree in spring, long before its variegated leaves appear.

The Temple

The latest addition to the gardens is the circular temple that now stands at the head of the Long Pond. It looks as if it has been there for ever, so well does it blend in.

The latest addition to the garden: a temple built by Philip Thomason

25

Lisa Roper, Mark's wife, had been wanting to put a dramatic feature here for many years. She finally set her heart on a temple, having come across the remnants of a similar broken-down building being repaired by a local potter, Philip Thomason, as she explains:

'He used Ham stone quarried out of the Ham Hills especially for us and the great coup was to put a pond in the centre that would reflect the wonderful wrought-iron roof, made by another craftsman locally. The whole thing is much better than I ever dreamed it would be. As soon as it went up it looked as if it should have been here all the time.'

Mark is full of admiration for his wife's brainwave: 'I honestly think it is the most lasting thing this family has done this century,' he declares.

And that is important to Mark, who takes his role as a custodian of Forde Abbey extremely seriously:

'I regard myself simply as a link in a chain, and you hope you're not a weak link, and that you can hand it on to the next lot, better perhaps than you found it. And I actually think, in today's world, with people coming round to pay to see the place, we have a better chance than previous generations perhaps did.'

EARLY SUMMER GARDENS

PAINSWICK ROCOCO GARDEN

The Stables, Painswick House, Painswick
Gloucestershire GL6 6TH. Tel. 01452 813204
Chairman, Painswick Rococo Garden Trust: Lord Dickinson;
Manager: Paul Moir

LOCATION
On the B4073 half a mile (800 metres) from the centre of Painswick.

VISITING
Open Wed.–Sun. from second Wed. in January to 30 November,
11am–5pm, daily during July and August, and Bank Holidays. Parties
by appointment. Admission: adults £3, over-60s £2.70, children £1.60.

FACILITIES
Coffee, lunches and teas in the licensed Coach House
Restaurant Wed.–Sun. Shop.

KEY FEATURES
Unique rococo-style garden
Children's Nature Trail
Nursery with rare plants

*The Rococo Garden has reached a milestone in its history. It was created in
1748 and this year is its 250th anniversary. It is great cause for celebration,
because none of us in our lifetime will ever see anything like it made again.*
(Paul Moir)

The Painswick Rococo Garden is thought to be the only complete garden of this style left in Britain. The rococo style of garden design briefly came to eminence from 1720 to 1760.

The word rococo is derived from two French words: *rocaille*, meaning 'rock work' and *coquille*, 'shell'. It is an allusion to oddly shaped groups of rocks, seashells and other natural forms artistically laid out in scrolls and the shapes of a capital 'C' and 'S'. The style is distinguished by asymmetry and a lack of visible balance between one element and another. Paul Moir, who runs the garden on behalf of the Trust that has been set up to fund it, has become something of an authority on the subject:

'The rococo period was a time when gardens were changing. Prior to it they had been quite formal and after it came the typical English landscape garden. In the rococo period you got aspects of both, the formal vistas competing with serpentine, woodland paths in a relatively limited area, with a mixture of building styles from the Classical to the Gothic, Doric and Rustic. There was a lot of experimentation and some rather strange, flamboyant decoration that reflected the lighthearted atmosphere of the times.'

Restoration

By visiting the garden now an immediate picture can be gained of what the rococo style is. However, this has only been possible for just over a decade. Until 1984, the garden, which lies in a sheltered, hidden combe behind Painswick House, lay buried beneath an overgrown wood.

All that remained to give any hint of what lay below the wood was a remarkable painting of the garden dated 1748 by Thomas Robins. There is a theory that it was Robins himself who designed the garden and that the painting was a proposal for the consideration of his patron. This painting was included in an exhibition of Robins' work staged in 1976, following which there was a resurgence of interest in gardens of the early eighteenth century and the realization of the national historic importance of the garden at Painswick. So in 1984 Lord Dickinson decided to embark on restoring the garden to its original form, and the bulldozers moved in to begin work.

'We saw that a complete restoration was possible since the garden had never been changed in fashion,' Paul explains. 'Nothing had been added at a later date, so we could go right back to 1748 using the very unusual painting that was almost painted as a plan, as though Robins had been up in a hot air balloon looking down on it. '

At every stage archaeologists were sent in to investigate and each time they came back with confirmation that the detail of the Robins painting was indeed correct.

However, the scale of the project began to escalate as costs far outstripped the original estimates and in 1988 a registered charity, the Painswick Rococo Garden Trust, was set up to oversee the rest of the restoration. Paul Moir, Lord Dickinson's stepson, was brought in to run it.

'One of the benefits of doing this was to ensure the garden will remain open for future generations, which it may not have done if it had continued to be run on a private basis,' he comments.

The Red House

A shady, wooded path leads into the valley where the garden is located. The first building that greets you is rather a startling one, and gives an immediate impression of the kind of features that lie in store in the rest of the garden. The Red House has a curious asymmetrical façade. It looks as though

The Red House

it should have a third wing, but none was ever intended. The building has been carefully restored using traditional lime plaster exactly in accordance with eighteenth-century methods. The exterior is coloured with a bright red lime wash, for reasons Paul makes clear:

'The last thing you would expect to see in a garden built in the Cotswolds, where there is plenty of lovely Cotswold stone, is a building made to look like it is built out of almost London red brick. But it goes back to the idea of the surprise they tried to build in. And also it does stand out from the bottom of the garden.'

From the Red House there are three different vistas over the garden, including the main one down the central avenue.

The Exedra

In May and June the area at the top of the garden, known as the Exedra, reached via a serpentine path, is a sea of rippling blooms. Tall spires of foxgloves stretch up among love-in-a-mist, poppies, iris, sweet rocket, and a mass of other plants thought to have been grown in the eighteenth century. The term Exedra means 'an outside seating area or discussion place', and certainly this would be a great place to sit, relax and gossip! The two bedding areas are enclosed by low fences and edged with honeysuckle dripping from thick ropes looped between upright posts, and a splendidly bizarre façade rises up behind.

Apart from the Robins painting, there was no evidence of this architectural phenomenon at all, and so it has been re-created from scratch, just as it would have been in the eighteenth century. For this one item, the bill totalled a staggering £35,000, which gives some indication of the sort of costs involved in restoration work of this kind. Again traditional materials such as laths and plaster have been used, and the whole structure is reinforced with a central core of steel to stop it being blown over in the wind. The shape is not unlike a semi-circular crown, with raised points on the top and six arches on the bottom. The whole makes a wonderfully romantic and quirky picture when seen reflected in the circular pond at its feet or from various points across the garden.

PAUL'S EIGHTEENTH-CENTURY EXEDRA FAVOURITES

Hyssopus officinalis	Blue, white or pink
Ranunculus asiaticus	Buttercup; double varieties, various colours

*In the eighteenth century the Exedra garden was
a good outdoor spot to sit and talk.*

Nigella damascena	Love-in-a-mist; wispy blue
Asphodelus albus	White asphodel; star-shaped flowers
Hesperis matronalis	*Sweet rocket*; white flower spikes

The Kitchen Garden

Below the Exedra lies the geometrically designed Kitchen Garden. Its overall plan is best viewed from higher up on the sides of the valley. A myriad of paths transect the area, dividing it into many asymmetrical vegetable plots filled with the types of produce thought to have been available 200 years ago. Every path was found to be exactly where Robins' painting suggested and, as in the picture, each has been bordered with old varieties of apples and pears trained as espaliers.

The geometric pattern of the Kitchen Garden has been recreated following Robins' 1748 painting.

The beds radiated out from a central pond that is also original, although it needed much work to render it sound and waterproof again.

The Plunge Pool

The gentlemen of the eighteenth century must have been hardier folk than we are today! Apparently when the heat got too much they simply stripped off and plunged into the ice-cold pool at the bottom of the garden that is fed by a stream rushing down from the Cotswolds. This was thought to be good for the health. Today no one is brave enough to put the theory to the test and the pool merely acts as a reminder of times gone past.

The Eagle House

If you glance up to the opposite side of the valley, another typically rococo-style building catches your eye. This is the Eagle House (the origin of its name is unknown). Its restoration has been another great achievement, because when work began nothing remained at all of the hexagonal top storey. However, the archeological evidence uncovered was far more informative than anyone dared hope, and so the resurrection of the curious building began. As with the Red House, the outer layer of plaster (with animal hair mixed in following the old methods), is painted with brilliant red, making it another spectacle that cannot be missed.

Other Features

The winding paths and straight avenues that lead around the garden take the visitor past a number of other features. These are of a variety of architectural forms, as befits the rococo style.

There is the Doric Seat, for example, standing guard to

*A glimpse of the Doric seat beyond
the flowers of the Exedra*

All the plants used in the garden are, as far as possible, varieties thought to be typical of the 1700s. Many of them are plants still frequently in use now.

PAUL'S FAVOURITE SHRUBS OF THE EIGHTEENTH CENTURY

Viburnum opulus	Guelder rose; white flower; leaves redden in autumn
Cornus alba	Red-barked dogwood; red stems in winter
Philadelphus coronarius	Mock orange; sweet-scented white flowers
Cotinus coggygria	Smoke tree; green leaves, red in autumn; mist of white flowers
Laburnum anagyroides	Common laburnum; deciduous tree with yellow flower clusters

one side of the Exedra, and the Gothic Alcove, another restoration success story, which can be found at the head of the Beech Walk. Behind the Alcove is the start of the children's nature trail, and from here steps also lead down into the Grove, an area that is carpeted with snowdrops in early spring. The snowdrops have been here for well over a hundred years. There are several varieties, but one of them, *Galanthus nivalis atkinsii*, may have been acquired from the noted nineteenth-century snowdrop grower, James Atkins, who once lived in Painswick.

The Pigeon House, with its unusual octagonal upper storey, stands on the far boundary of the garden and is believed to be the place from where Thomas Robins painted the garden.

Lord Dickinson himself admits that when he first embarked upon the restoration of the Painswick Rococo Garden he could never have imagined what an enormous undertaking it was to become, or indeed how it would influence his life. He now travels the world lecturing on the project. Back at home, running the enterprise on a daily basis, Paul Moir is delighted that the main restoration work is nearly complete:

'The garden has come full circle. It is almost back to its spring. It is being reborn just as it was in the early eighteenth century.'

SNAPE COTTAGE

(Private garden)

Angela and Ian Whinfield

Chaffeymoor, Bourton, Dorset SP8 5BY

Tel. 01747 840330 (evenings only)

LOCATION

Take the B3081 Bourton exit off the A303. Then follow signs for Bourton. Take the
second left off the main road into Bourton, go up the hill past Abbey Plants,
and Snape Cottage is at the top on a sharp left-hand bend.

VISITING

Garden open every Wed. and Sun. in April, May June, July and September, 2–5pm.
(Closed August.) Last two Suns in February and Mother's Day for snowdrops and
hellebores. Admission: £1.50. Parties by appointment.

FACILITIES

Cream teas (pre-booked groups only). Unusual plants and iron plant supports for sale;
also rustic furniture. Bed and Breakfast for garden lovers. Unsuitable for wheelchairs.

KEY FEATURES

Plantsman's half-acre (0.2-hectare) country garden
Old-fashioned and unusual perennials and many native plants
Wildlife interest
Hot, dry border
Pond
Wild-flower area
Medieval garden
Hurdle making

*My main philosophy is really to plant everything in the place it would prefer to grow, taking
account of colour, form and texture while also making the garden look as natural as it can.*
(Angela Whinfield)

Angela's garden is proof that it is possible to have an attractive garden which is also beneficial to wildlife.

As you round the bend approaching Snape Cottage it is obvious there is a garden lover within, for the walls outside and the bed bordering the road are a mass of foliage and flowers. Many of the plants are simply hedgerow plants allowed to grow in wild profusion, an early sign that the person who lives here is very much at one with our native species.

Snape Cottage is, as Angela Whinfield herself explains, 'Small enough for people to relate to. It is not outside most people's aspirations to do what we are doing here.'

Indeed, there are so many different areas created in the garden that it is a great place to go to see ideas being put into practice. And it all has a picturesque cottagey feel that is immediately warm and welcoming.

Angela and her husband Ian came here thirteen years ago from the suburbs of Harrow. Their seemingly idyllic country life now is a far cry from their previous existence, in which Angela was a secretary for Coca-Cola and Ian was a painter and decorator. Ian is now a self-taught furniture and hurdle maker and Angela is devoted full time to the garden. She too has learnt everything from scratch, as she admits:

'I wasn't very good at school but everything I have learnt about gardening is really self-taught. I've had no formal training and I think this is certainly the best way for someone like me to learn. The gardening I do here is completely experimental. I also learn from the visitors, by exchanging experiences.'

The Pond

From a young age Angela had an interest in natural history, and that has greatly influenced what she is trying to achieve at Snape Cottage. She is very conscious of the habitats that are being lost in the wild, and is keen to redress the balance by introducing wild flowers into her garden and recreating different habitats that are disappearing from the countryside.

She has been much inspired by Chris Baines' book *How to Make a Wildlife Garden*. His recommendations on how to develop a wildlife pond have been carried out to perfection by Angela. The pond takes pride of place in front of the house and looks as natural as can be. No concrete edges, no plastic showing and no goldfish! (They are an absolute sin in a true wildlife pond, because they eat all the dragonfly larvae.) The pond, developed over a natural spring, blends almost imperceptibly into the lawn. It is planted up with native species such as the bog bean, lady's smock and the striking yellow flag iris.

'It is such a reward to see how quickly it was colonized and what a great diversity of wildlife uses the pond,' Angela remarks. 'Particularly interesting are the varieties of damsel- and dragonflies that breed here; also the palmate newts and diving beetles.'

And while we were filming much excitement was caused by the spotting of a rare great crested newt – for the first time ever in this pond!

ANGELA'S FAVOURITE POND PLANTS

Menyanthes trifoliata	Bog bean; white flower
Cardamine pratensis	Lady's smock; pinkish white flower
Caltha palustris	Marsh marigold; golden yellow flower
Lychnis flos-cuculi	Ragged Robin; pink, fringed flower
Iris pseudacorus	Yellow flag iris

The Herbaceous Borders

Whereas it was Chris Baines who influenced Angela's wildlife leanings, it was Margery Fish, through her book *Cottage Garden Flowers*, who really got Angela into gardening in the first place. She told us:

'The book has had a major influence on my life, because it encouraged me to try and collect as many of the old varieties of garden plants as I could and to put them in the right place for them so that they would thrive in their natural conditions.'

Angela has plenty of scope to try a range of plants in different locations, since she has a hot, dry border, a boggy border where an underground spring runs, the sunny south side of the cottage, and the shady north-facing border alongside the road. And Angela is meticulous in determining the best possible spot for each of her plants:

'Whenever I get a plant that's new to me I always look it up in as many reference books as I can and get different ideas and opinions on it to see where it would prefer to grow. I never plant anything until I feel fairly happy that I am going to get it right first time. And in fact I don't often have to move plants.'

In May many plants are already in their full glory in the Boggy Border. They are grouped not simply according to interest; they must also look good together in terms of their colour and texture. And you need not worry about plant identification in this garden; every plant is carefully labelled!

ANGELA'S BOGGY BORDER FAVOURITES

Ranunculus aconitifolius 'Flore Pleno'	Double white buttercup
Filipendula ulmaria 'Aurea'	Golden meadow-sweet; bright gold leaves
Carex elata 'Aurea'	Bowles' golden sedge; gold foliage with green margins
Eupatorium purpureum subsp. *maculatum* 'Atropurpureum'	Hemp agrimony; dark form
Cirsium rivulare atropurpureum	Ruby red thistle

The Medieval Garden

Another of Angela's interests is the history of plants. This is beautifully illustrated in the novel medieval-style garden area she has created, neatly surrounded by hazel hurdles and archways made by her husband Ian. The area contains a mass of plants that in the fourteenth century would have had

The Medieval Garden, bounded by Ian Whinfield's handmade hazel hurdles

particular uses. Initially one is drawn in by some of the delightful scents emanating from the garden, in particular the strong smell of coconut coming from the brilliant yellow double gorse bush. Lavenders and lemon balm are other scent-givers.

Almost every plant here has a story attached to it. For example, the root of the *Iris florentina* (or orris root, as it was known) was dried and ground up to make a fixative for pot pourri and pomanders. The roots of Solomon's seal were pulverized to make a poultice said to reduce freckles and blemishes of the skin. And an important blue dye was extracted from the plant woad.

ANGELA'S FAVOURITES FOR A MEDIEVAL GARDEN

Iris germanica var. *florentina*	Orris root iris; May
Polygonatum odoratum	Solomon's seal; white bell-like flowers
Isatis tinctoria	Woad; yellow cluster of flowers on each head
Valeriana officinalis	Scented, soft pinky lilac; 5 feet (1.5 metres) tall
Rosa gallica var. *officinalis*	Strident pink rose

The Woodland Edge

Beyond the Medieval Garden you are drawn into a flowery woodland bower via a mown grassy path beneath blossoming apple trees that rise out of wild grasses. Here at the bottom of the garden, where it blends gently into the surrounding landscape, Angela has tried to recreate a woodland-edge habitat. It is one that is fast disappearing in the wild and can provide a home to a large number of insects and invertebrates. Like many other parts of the garden, it is still in the experimental stages.

Already the bluebells have been succeeded by lacy cow parsley and deep-pink campions are forming an eye-catching backdrop. Angela intends to add to the diversity by introducing more wild plants into the rough grass in the form of seedling plugs.

'I try to get across to people that weeds are actually beautiful plants in their own right,' she says. 'A weed is simply a plant in the wrong place, but a weed in the right place can look fantastic, like the cow parsley, knapweed and scabious.'

Although this woodland area may look wild, the key to its appearance is actually to manage it correctly. It must be mown at the right time to suit the flowering and seeding of the required plants. At the moment this is done in late June.

The wild woodland-edge area at the bottom of the garden

ANGELA'S FAVOURITES FOR WOODLAND EDGES

Anthriscus sylvestris	Cow parsley; tall with lacy white flowers
Silene dioica	Campion; deep pink
Centaurea scabiosa	Greater knapweed; reddish magenta flowers
Saxifraga granulata	Meadow saxifrage; creamy white flowers

The garden that Angela and Ian have evolved between them, Angela with her plant knowledge and Ian with his manual skills, has been developed very much on a shoestring. Many of the first plants came from tiny scraps given by friends, and now each of these plants has its own special memory attached to it.

It is important to Angela that people continue to come and visit Snape Cottage and share in a little of her own pleasure in it, and perhaps learn something from it along the way, as she makes clear:

'Some people who come are plant fanatics, and go around studying everything. Others just enjoy sitting and absorbing the atmosphere. It doesn't matter, as long as people enjoy their garden – or our garden, or any garden. That is the main thing.'

The Whinfields take a break on Ian's rustic furniture.

STANCOMBE PARK

Gerda Barlow

Dursley, Gloucestershire GL1l 6AU

Tel. 01453 542815

LOCATION

3 miles (5 km) from Dursley and Wotton-under-Edge,
off the B4060, signposted Stancombe.

VISITING

Group tours given by appointment only; admission: £3 per person.

FACILITIES

Teas served in the conservatory on request. Austrian cakes a speciality.
Lower garden not suitable for wheelchairs.

KEY FEATURES

Upper garden with formal ornamental beds and topiary
Secret lower 'Folly Garden' with lake, temple, Egyptian and Chinese areas
Picturesque Cotswold Valley

*When I first came here I thought it was paradise, although in those
days it was pretty neglected and not very much loved, but the setting is so
beautiful my late husband Basil and I fell in love with it straight away.*

(Gerda Barlow)

Stancombe Park is located in its own little piece of the Cotswolds. The Park lies at the head of a quintessentially English valley, which has steeply sloping sides where Gerda's own cattle graze and is bordered at the top by luxuriously verdant broadleaved woodland surrounding the famous Gloucestershire landmark of Stinchcombe Hill.

The house stands on a promontory at the head of the valley and, unusually, the upper garden is set several hundred yards away from the house, allowing one of the spurs of the valley to protrude between it and the garden.

The Baroque swirls and curves of the Patterned Border

Austrian-born Gerda Barlow

Strangely enough, it has the effect of setting the garden off in rather a grand style.

And if the setting is captivating, so is the lady of the house herself. With a beaming smile and a twinkle in her eye, Gerda Barlow makes visitors instantly welcome. Her Austrian accent is still dominant after a lifetime of living in England, having married what she openly describes as an archetypal English gentleman. Even the lilt of Gerda's speech adds to the uniqueness and the attraction of Stancombe.

The Upper Garden

When you enter the Upper Garden, the eye is drawn first to a view from the terrace back to the house and across the valley. This brings home the importance, when the garden was designed, of ensuring that it blended into its magnificent setting.

The floor of the terrace itself is interesting, as it is a replica of a section of a Roman mosaic found on the estate. Two original panels of the mosaic can be seen set into the wall in the courtyard.

After expounding on the views, Gerda turns with delight to her latest creation in the garden, of which she is justly proud. This is the Patterned Border, which was put in only eight years ago, to replace some very old herbaceous borders. By now the intricately interwoven pattern of topiary is so well established it looks as if it has always been here. The design was drawn up in detail on graph paper with the aid of garden designer Nada Jennett.

'Being Austrian, I like the Baroque influence with its swirls and curves,' Gerda tells us. 'The patterns look particularly effective in the winter touched with hoarfrost.'

The symmetrical borders lie on either side of a central walkway. The hedging is of yew, box, holly and euonymous, all neatly clipped to perfection. The patterns are infilled with a variety of plants ranging from the cold colours such as blue and grey to warmer tones of lime greens and reds.

Doing away with the former herbaceous borders was a momentous decision for Gerda, but now she wouldn't be without this new development.

GERDA'S FAVOURITES FOR COLOUR IN THE PATTERNED BORDER
BLUE

Eucalyptus gunnii	Cider gum; silver-blue leaves, peeling bark
Hosta 'Bressingham Blue'	Plaintain lily; bluish

43

	decorative foliage
Agapanthus Headbourne Hybrids	Trumpet-shaped flowers
Festuca glauca	Blue fescue; tuft-forming perennial grass
Lilium regale	Lily; summer-flowering bulb

RED

Cotinus coggygria 'Royal Purple'	Deciduous shrub; purple-red leaves, deep pink flower plumes
Sedum trolii 'Vera Johnson'	Stonecrop; fleshy
Heuchera micrantha 'Palace Purple'	Perennial; deep purple, heart-shaped leaves, white flowers
Ajuga reptans 'Atropurpurea'	Evergreen, ground-cover perennial; bronze/purple leaves
Alium karataviense	Spring-flowering bulb; pale pink spherical flower-head

The Circular Garden

Leaving the Patterned Border, it is the simple circles surrounding a huge Italian urn that next attract attention. Again, shape and simplicity have proved a winning combination. The urn came from the great garden collection of Sir Francis Cooke. It has been raised up in the centre of a circular bed filled with bright lilies in the summer and edged with more box hedging. The whole effect is complemented by an outer circle of the bright golden foliage of *Acer pseudoplatanus* 'Worleei', the golden sycamore. (You cannot miss the two deep-bronze impostors that have crept into this circle as well; they arrived by mistake, but Gerda thought it would be fun to include them anyway!)

The final relish in this area is given by the under-planting of deep purple *Allium hollandicum*, interspersed with the metallic hues of the *Rosa rubrifolia* leaves.

The circular bed, as well as the pleached hornbeam walk which leads from two stone cherubs and a well-placed bench for viewing the scene, all bear the hallmark of Gerda's influence. As she explains:

'I always thought simplicity is the answer, and colour and form. I think it is much more effective if you keep it simple, not crowded with all sorts of plants and colours. Colours need to be kept to a harmonious effect.'

The Valley Walk

For the next part of the tour be ready for a surprise, and a walk! Leaving the upper garden on a shady track through the wood, you come out on a grassy walkway that skirts the side of the valley. The scene of the steep valley edged with buttercups and dotted with cattle is breathtaking, and never fails to inspire Gerda even after all these years:

'It is a fantastic view. And the mood changes so often. In the evening it is so different to the morning. I always get emotional about it. I am so lucky to be a custodian of this lovely bit of England.'

With a girlish laugh, Gerda delights in pointing out the topiary animals that line the 'menagerie walk' on the way to the lake at the bottom of the valley. It is great fun to spot the squirrel, the gorilla and, cutest of all, the pig with its squat snout.

After about a quarter of a mile (400 metres), the path turns into a series of steep stone steps that descend into a wooded area, and soon gushing water can be seen springing from the hillside. The path takes a sharp turn and leads past an alcove in which nestles a stone font, overflowing with water. This is another of the garden's Roman remains. All the while the way is getting more overgrown and the suspense is building. At last the path narrows and leads directly into a narrow, dark tunnel with a stone guard-dog at the entrance.

And it is now that Gerda is drawn to recount the extraordinary tale of the Reverend David Edwards, who lived at Stancombe early last century. It was he who created the Folly Garden, legend has it, to carry out his secret liaison with a local gypsy girl. It was believed that his wife, the former Miss Purnell, who was a wealthy but stout lady, was unlikely to walk the distance to this far part of the garden. Even if she did, it is said that the narrow paths would have deterred her further; the tunnels were impassable, being kept padlocked!

Mrs Purnell-Edwards, however, missed out on a wonderful spectacle that has now been listed by English Heritage as a Grade I garden. On emerging from the series of tunnels one is met with a romantic view across a wide lake, edged with a

In Stancombe's Egyptian garden

long stone pathway on one side and a grand copper beech drooping to the water's edge on the other. And still there are more surprises in store. The path leads on through an Egyptian area where a whalebone arch marks the entrance to an ice-house, and then one comes face to face with the *pièce de résistance*: a perfect temple on the other side of the lake. With a grant from English Heritage this has been sympathetically restored; indeed, the Reverend would have been proud of it.

It was Gerda's son Nic, also passionate about the garden, who took on the task of restoring the temple, intending to return it somehow to its original purpose, that of a love nest! And now that it is completed he plans to hire the temple out to honeymoon couples. A more romantic setting would be hard to find. The temple has its claim to fame: it was here that Evelyn Waugh often sat writing, and he is believed to have based some of the settings of *Brideshead Revisited* on this garden.

The Barlows have worked tirelessly to restore the Folly Garden to the condition Waugh would have enjoyed. Over the years it had fallen into a sad state of neglect.

'We couldn't even find the paths at first,' recalls Gerda. 'It was great fun making new discoveries, but it was a vast job.'

Despite her age, she trots up and down from the main

The temple in the Grade I listed Folly Garden was recently restored for honeymooning couples.

house to the Folly Garden, sometimes three times a day, and when she gets here there is always something to do and something to plan. All the work in the two areas of garden is carried out entirely by Gerda's faithful gardener, Richard Eastwood, and herself. Given the vast expanse of the place, it is definitely a labour of love.

'It is a lot of work,' she agrees, 'but I believe that if you get involved physically and really work hard then you get extra-ordinary satisfaction and that is worth everything.'

MID-SUMMER GARDENS

THE PETO GARDEN, IFORD MANOR

Elizabeth Cartwright-Hignett

Iford Manor, Iford, near Bradford-on-Avon
Wiltshire BM 5 2BA. Tel. 01225 863146

LOCATION
7 miles (11 km) south of Bath on the AS6. From Bradford-on-Avon and
Trowbridge; approach via the village of Westwood.
Entrance to the gardens from Iford bridge only.

VISITING
Open May–September, daily except Mon. and Fri., 2–5pm; April–
October, Suns 2–5pm. Also Easter. Parties by appointment. Admission:
adults £2.50, OAPs, students and children £1.90, children under ten free.

FACILITIES
Teas only, May–August on Sat., Sun. and Bank Holidays.
Dogs must be on leads. Not suitable for wheelchairs.

KEY FEATURES
Italian-style garden created by Harold Peto
Colonnades, terraces, cloisters, statues, ponds

*It is an absolute privilege to live here and every time I look
out of the door I think, How come I live in a place as
beautiful as this? But it is a great deal of hard work.'*
(Elizabeth Cartwright-Hignett)

Elizabeth Cartwright-Hignett came to Iford Manor thirty-five years ago. She describes how, when she first came here, although the whole garden and even the valley in which it is set were wildly overgrown, she fell in love with the place, knowing quite well that it would be a lifetime's undertaking to put it all together again.

To step into the garden at Iford is to step into a little bit of Italy. And while Iford has Roman roots, the romantic Italian style the garden exudes is attributed almost entirely to a previous owner, Harold Ainsworth Peto, who bought the house in 1899 and lived here for thirty-three years.

Harold Peto

Peto was an architect by profession and a partner of Sir Ernest George, who built much of the area around Kensington and Chelsea. Sir Edwin Lutyens became a pupil

Terracing is a major feature at Iford, because the garden has been created on a steep hillside.

of Peto and was highly influenced by Peto's ideas. Peto himself became increasingly interested in garden design during the later part of his life and undertook numerous commissions, the best know being Buscott Park (now owned by the National Trust), Hartham Park, Wayford Manor and Ilnacullin Island in Bantry Bay, as well as several gardens on the Continent.

Since taking over Iford, Elizabeth and her husband John have become steeped in Peto culture and history. Elizabeth explains what it was that so attracted him to the Italian designs:

'Although an architect, Peto had an interest in gardens, particularly the Italian style, because he felt that gardens should have an architectural basis so they looked good all the year round, and the old Italian gardens are the classic examples of that idea. In them the flowers occupy a subordinate place amongst the cypresses, broad walks, statues and pools.'

Iford was indeed Peto's dream country house and garden. It was a setting in which he could try out his ideas and where he could make use of his collection of antique fragments.

The garden was in a very dilapidated state when Elizabeth took it over. At first she battled with the restoration aided by the trusty hand of gardener Leon Butler, and later she was also joined by husband John. There are parts of the garden that are not attributed to Peto, but the main body is a remarkable testament of his skill, of which, as Elizabeth says, they are only too aware:

'I think we both feel that we are curators of someone else's design. It was a wonderful design, he had a remarkable eye, and I think it is our job to look after it.'

The Lower Terraces

Entering the garden through a wrought-iron gate at the

south-east corner of the house, you come to the Loggia. Water spills from a lion-mask fountain in a pretty semi-circular pool in the paved courtyard and straight away the Italian atmosphere is apparent. Everywhere statues and architectural features tell of Peto's love. There is an Italian Renaissance window set into the Loggia, and a bas-relief head of a boy of the Medici family.

Steps take you up to a second terrace, where there is a conservatory and another flight of steps leads up to the lawn. A pair of grand marble lions of Italian workmanship dating from about 1200 stand guard at the bottom of these steps.

Terracing is a prominent feature of the garden, which is set into a steep hillside. Much of the stonework in the garden has had to be underpinned to prevent it slipping down the hill. In this John has had to become something of an expert:

'A lot of the stonework was very shaky and the hillside is a bit like an escalator: it moves all the time, being alternate layers of stone and clay and well fed with streams that run out at intervals. So the walls have had to be especially under-pinned.'

From the top of the steps you can branch off onto another path that leads to a further series of terraces to the left, which are again adorned with statuary and urns trailing flowers.

The Great Terrace

The Great Terrace is the central feature of the garden. The long straight walkway (now gravelled, but originally paved), is lined with regal columns and statues, many of which Peto brought back from Italy and which are of significant his-torical interest. Elizabeth never tires of talking about this work of art:

'Peto had the idea that the terrace should end in a kind of outdoor basilica. So he created the apse with the rounded

seat at one end, and various rooms off the terrace like side chapels. One of these is the Blue Pool Garden, where the yew hedges have been clipped into the shape of the crest of the Chigi family of Siena in memory of my grandmother, who was a member of that family. Another of the rooms leading from the Great Terrace is the Cloister Garth with its own paved terrace.'

Situated in the Cloister Garth is a captivating building called the Casita. It has exceptionally tall Verona columns of fine pink marble at the entrance and is very much an Italian building. However, if you look carefully at the wood at the top of the columns it is obvious that some Japanese influence has crept in, which gives a hint of Peto's other great love: that of Japan.

The Japanese Garden

John may be found working anywhere in the garden, but it is not unusual to find him loitering beneath the dappled shade cast by the acers in the Japanese garden. In modern times the idea of the Japanese garden has become an often overworked concept, but this Peto-devised Japanese garden seems to capture what they are really all about. Although the garden contains the standard two lanterns, a temple and a Buddha, it seems to achieve a peace and an atmosphere seldom found in other Japanese gardens.

Much of the credit for the overall image must be given to the current owners, however, for they have completed the garden that Peto never quite finished, introducing the water that previously would not run. While sifting out weed from the pond John tells us something of the garden's history:

'Peto was a great traveller, and in 1898 he went to Japan to see the cherries and maples, and he was totally overtaken by the place. He would have loved the formality of Japan,

View down to the pond from the Great Terrace

just as he loved the formality of Italian Renaissance gardens, and you can see that he has tried to combine the ideas.'

The Cloister

At the far end of the garden is a tranquil haven set slightly apart from the rest of the garden. This is the Cloister, built by Peto in 1914 partly to house the remaining antique fragments gathered on his travels, and partly as a historical continuation of the cloisters which once existed closer to the house. It is built in the Italian Romanesque style of about 1200, and while many of the decorative pieces have come from Italy, much of the building's impressive stonework was carried out by masons from the nearby village of Westwood.

Through the remarkably ornate ironwork gates can be seen a charming open court edged by twin columns. In this unique outdoor setting music recitals and plays are frequently performed.

Planting

No planting plans were available for Peto's garden, so the gardener, Leon Butler, has had to deduce what types of plants might have been used. He has been helped by finding many old plant labels left from Peto's day scattered about the borders. It seems the plants were mainly architectural in nature, with shape and form being more important than a riot of colour.

JOHN'S FAVOURITE PETO PLANTS

Wisteria sinensis	Chinese wisteria; racemes of pale violet flowers
Phillyrea angustifolia	Evergreen, dense shrub; dark green leaves, small greenish-white flowers
Buxus sempervirens	Common box; evergreen shrub; glossy, dark green leaves
Cupressus sempervirens	Italian cypress; narrow, upright conifer; grey-green foliage
Hemerocallis citrina	Perennial; large fragrant trumpet-shaped yellow flowers

100 Years of Peto

1999 will be a special year at Iford, for it will mark the centenary of Peto coming to the house and garden. Great celebrations are planned. The enthusiasm the Hignetts display for Peto remains undimmed, despite all the trials (not to mention the vast costs) the restoration of his work has presented, as John confirms:

'I just regard it as a privilege to be following in the path of a man who had the skill and the imagination to create something like this from virtually nothing. That's pretty good!'

John admits that he would loved to have met the man himself:

'It is said that Peto was irascible; he made his gardeners wear red sweaters so he could see whether they were bending down or not, and yet on the other hand he was apparently much admired, if not loved, by his family. He was also part of that Ruskinite set that gave an Englishness to the rapport between England and Italy, France and Spain. I would have loved to have been part of that, but of course it is too late now.'

However, simply to bask in Peto's reflected glory through the restoration of his garden is enough for Elizabeth Cartwright-Hignett. She sums up their experiences here:

'It has been an enormous task. A place like this is a black hole as far as expense is concerned, but it seems to me that it is worth doing and it has been enormous fun. We have

The Cloister

loved every minute of it, and despite the frustrations and difficulties and trying to finance it, it has been eminently worth doing.'

THE URN COTTAGE

(*Private garden*)

Dr Lesley Rosser

Charfield, Wotton-under-Edge, Gloucestershire GL12 8SY. Tel. 01453 843156

LOCATION

After exit 14 on the M5, take the B4509 to Wotton-under-Edge.
Turn left onto the B4058 to Charfield. In the village of Charfield turn
right into Station Road. The Urn Cottage is the last cottage on the left,
down a long track through a five-barred gate.

VISITING

Opening times as advertised in *Gardens of England and Wales Open
for Charity*, supported by the National Gardens Scheme
('The Yellow Book'). Groups by appointment.

FACILITIES

Teas by arrangement

Plant sales

Wheelchair access (phone to discuss)

KEY FEATURES

Garden designer's small cottage garden with variety of areas

Stream garden with plant amphitheatre

Sunny south-facing beds

Ornamental grass bed

Wild area including children's playhouse

Vegetable patch

*It definitely isn't a chore to come and work in my own garden after a day working in
someone else's garden. It is an absolute necessity, because for me it's a retreat from the
business of life and the pressures of work. It is just wonderful therapy to be able to
come home to my own garden and work away in it, free from the cares of the world.*

(Dr Lesley Rosser)

r Lesley Rosser is a garden designer and every day she plans gardens for other people, but she never tires of her own garden at The Urn Cottage. It was moving to this spot sixteen years ago and gradually developing the garden which made her realize what pleasure she got from tending the soil and to wonder whether it was time for a career change.

Until then Lesley had been a research scientist, but she decided to try her hand at making a living out of some aspect of gardening and so over a period of time she became a garden designer. She can now boast of being a Full Member and Council Member of the renowned Society of Garden Designers. She puts a lot of her success down to the experiences she has gained from her own garden. Here, with the skills of the scientist undoubtedly moulding her methods,

A salmon-pink Rosa 'Compassion' *scrambles up the stone front of the cottage.*

she experiments with plants and studies them in much detail before she feels confident to introduce them into other people's gardens.

'The garden has many different areas being treated in quite different ways,' she tells us. 'We're open and exposed on the south side, whereas on the north side we have a stream and quite large trees overhead where it is cool and shady. And the soil in the garden varies considerably throughout. In some places it is very shallow and in other places it is deeper. This means we can provide different sorts of planting in each area of the garden, so developing quite contrasting atmospheres.'

The half-acre (0.2-hectare) garden revolves around the pretty cottage, which has been tastefully extended in all directions. Even though there is such a range of areas to be found in the garden, they do not seem crammed in. The visitor moves almost imperceptibly from one part to another, at times looking inwards to the heart of the garden and at others being made aware of the wider picture with the dramatic backdrop of the Cotswold escarpment behind.

The Sunny South Side

A soft salmon-pink climbing rose (*Rosa* 'Compassion') adorns the front of the house, blending in harmoniously with the warm tones of the stonework. All the plants in this area thrive in hot, sunny conditions. In fact, the French lavender (*Lavandula stoechas*) and the silvery grey *Artemisia canescens* will not grow anywhere else in the garden, because it is too cold and essentially a frost pocket. However, against the south facing wall they are thriving.

The slightly tender pink *Geranium palmatum* is also quite happy here growing among the paving stones, which in retaining the heat act as a kind of storage heater for the

On the South Side of the garden the spongy, low-growing Raoulia australis *thrives among the paving stones alongside thymes and the pink* Geranium palmatum.

plants. Lesley has almost turned the path into a bed in itself, so many plants are bursting from between its stones, all of them tolerant, in varying degrees, of being trodden on! The spongy mass of the low-growing *Raoulia australis*, for example, is a great favourite with visitors; none can resist getting down on their hands and knees to smooth it. Many of the other plants are aromatic, such as the thymes.

FAVOURITE LOW-GROWING PLANTS FOR A PATH

Raoulia australis	Silver foliage; forms spongy mat
Geranium Sessiliflorum 'Nigricans'	Black-leaved geranium
Thymus Serpyllum albus	White, long-lasting thyme
Geranium palmatum	Pink geranium; keep to sides of path
Mentha requienii	Corsican mint; keep in shade

Before leaving the front of the house you notice the many plants spilling from the attractively planted terracotta pots and urns dotted about. There are pots discreetly placed all around the garden, aptly reflecting the name of the cottage.

The Grass Bed

Lesley openly admits that the large bed in front of the conservatory is an experimental one. Here she is trying out various grasses which are new to her, and among them she has planted an array of other flowers which will protrude up through the grasses at different times of the year.

'My favourite grass is the *Stipa tenuifolia*, which is very soft and flows gracefully in the breeze,' she says. 'Through that I am growing yellow alliums and blue flax will come up later. I am also delighted with the *Stipa gigantea*, which has been here quite some time and is now a stunning specimen.'

After much trial and error Lesley is also finding that among a range of grasses the purple heucheras with their richly coloured foliage work well, as do the yellow achilleas.

LESLEY'S FAVOURITE COMBINATIONS OF GRASSES AND FLOWERS

Stipa tenuifolia	Feathery grass
Stipa gigantea	Golden oat; large, gold-tinged seed-heads
Molinia caerulea	Green grass, orangey brown in autumn
Heuchera 'Chocolate Ruffles'	Purple stems, ivory flowers
Achillea 'Moonshine'	Yellow flowers
Allium obliquum	Yellow-green flower-head

The Vegetable Patch

A pergola, built by Lesley's husband and now completely

engulfed by foliage, forms an effective barrier between the Grass Bed and the family vegetable patch. Even this area has been well thought out and is in its own way attractive. The narrow terraced beds are edged entirely with railway sleepers and the pathways between them are also faced with sleepers. This layout was completed only two years ago, but is already clearly a great improvement on the traditional arrangement that pre-dated it on the steep slope, as Lesley explains:

'Now I can work in my vegetable areas from the paths on either side of the beds, and I can come down here without putting on my boots. My children can come and garden with me and help harvest and weed, too. So it has made life very easy.'

The patch provides virtually all the vegetables and soft fruit the family of four needs for the whole year. The summer's surplus is frozen for the winter and there are always a few surprises to sample, such as the Japanese onions and leaf vegetables Lesley is trying out using some seed sent by a Japanese visitor who came to the garden a few years ago. The whole area is meticulously tidy, and prettied up with a sprinkling of flowers. Lesley says:

'I try to make the area look as attractive as possible with the addition of some ornamental planting, such as the foxtail lilies growing amongst the asparagus and annuals like the poached-egg plant and lovely red poppies. Not only does this look good, it is beneficial for the insects too.'

The Stream Bed

There is an outdoor eating area on the north side of the house where meals can be taken in the shade on hot summer's days. Crossing the lawn you arrive at the gushing stream that forms the boundary to this side of the garden. The circular lawn, although small, does a good job in providing a feeling of space in what is actually quite a narrow part of the garden. Since the land slopes away here, the circle of the lawn is on a tilt which, interestingly, is usually considered incorrect in garden-design terms. However, Lesley thinks it works well here and so she has happily gone against convention.

By the stream an unusual area has been created that makes the best use of what might be considered tricky conditions, especially since the stream is liable to flooding. At the bottom of the shady bank by the stream edge, moisture-loving plants such as the ostrich feather fern (*Matteuccia struthiopteris*), the variegated flag iris (*Iris pseudocorus* 'Variegata') and various primulas thrive, being kept evenly moist by water coming from an upturned urn. The terracotta urn cleverly siphons water from the stream, and no electricity is needed.

Pottery urns are a trademark of the garden.

Above this bottom section tiered beds have been formed in a circular manner, rather like an amphitheatre for plants! On it plants that like moist but well-draining conditions (because of the slope) are growing very happily. The north-facing aspect means that moisture is retained on the plants' roots but their tops still receive some sunshine. Surprisingly, a lot of plants like these quite refined conditions and do extraordinarily well here, especially when helped along by Lesley's husbandry techniques:

'It is essential to dig in lots of good garden compost to the beds between the stones and to add mulch every year. The humus levels must be kept high in order to suck up the moisture.'

LESLEY'S FAVOURITES FOR A MOIST, WELL-DRAINED, SUNNY AREA

Corydalis flexuosa 'China Blue'	Soft blue, nodding head
Carex elata 'Aurea'	Golden grass
Hakonechloa macra 'Aureola'	Gold and green foliage
Dicentra formosa 'Oregona'	White flower, blue foliage
Iris sibirica 'Sky Wings'	Pale blue

The Wild Area

Now the tour takes the visitor away from the conventional parts of the garden around the house (passing both gold and purple borders), to the end of the garden. The lovely views of the Cotswold escarpment open up again and against the wonderful panoramic views a wild garden area has been developed, giving the impression of merging almost imperceptibly into the landscape beyond. Here the grass is allowed to grow long and wild flowers have been encouraged. A few paths have been mown through the grass so that the children can get to their swings and the charming tree-house.

Like many of the other gardeners we met who have tried to create a wild area, Lesley has found that it is not as simple as it looks:

'It is easy to achieve an element of wilderness by letting some of the grasses grow long and mowing paths through them, but to get a bit of additional interest in the area is quite hard work. The cow parsley came by itself, but to introduce the campion I had to grow it from seed and plant out the small plants. I have encouraged some types of buttercup, although I have removed the rampant creeping buttercup. So some considerable work has gone into extending the interest in the way of flowers.'

However, Lesley is now satisfied that the overall effect is appreciated by the whole family:

'This area of the garden has a very different feel to the rest of the garden. And although it is managed it is a very different management to the other areas. This is the end of the garden to escape into and the place where my children have great fun and get lost in the long grass.'

At The Urn Cottage, Lesley has created a garden of many atmospheres and moods, and it is a garden that can be enjoyed all year round. While she obviously creates gardens of a multitude of styles for other people in the course of her work as a designer, what she has developed here is what she wants for herself and her family. She is only too aware that gardens are very personal:

'I think people should develop their own gardens as their own patch. I don't think it is fair to exert any more influence on them than that. I do strongly believe gardens are for the people who live in them.'

LOWER SEVERALLS

Howard and Audrey Pring and Mary Cooper

Lower Severalls Garden and Nursery
Crewkerne, Somerset TA18 7NX
Tel. 0146073234

LOCATION
One and a half miles (2.5 km) north-east of Crewkerne on the
road between Merriott and Haselbury Plucknett.

OPENING
1 March–20 October, 10am–5pm daily except Thurs., Sun. 2pm–5pm.
Admission: adults £1.50, children free. Groups by appointment.

FACILITIES
Teas for pre-arranged groups. Wheelchair access

KEY FEATURES
Eighteenth-century Ham stone farmhouse
2.5 acres (1 hectare) of mixed borders and island beds
Dry riverbed (wadi) border
Living willow basket feature
Pond and bog garden
Nursery specializing in herbaceous perennials and herbs

*Farmers' wives bring their husbands to see me because farmers are generally
not good gardeners, and they ask me to tell them how I did all this. And I say,
'Well, just take in a little bit [of field] first. That is how I got started. I started
with a little bit and then got hooked on this garden design and I was done for!*

(Howard Pring)

Lower Severalls, surrounded by burgeoning summer beds

It was only when Howard Pring retired from farming twelve years ago that he really got into gardening. It has now become his all-consuming passion. The garden began as just the small rectangular area in front of the mellow, honey-coloured Ham stone eighteenth-century farmhouse. Since Howard has thrown himself into his new-found hobby it has grown to encompass an ever-increasing part of the field beyond. Every time he gets bored, he introduces a new border!

Howard has not been alone in his activities. It was initially his wife Audrey who was the master gardener:

'I have always loved the garden,' she says, 'ever since I got married fifty years ago. And we love going off for weekends and touring around plant nurseries and having a lovely time buying up more plants.'

And it doesn't end there, for gardening at Lower Severalls has become very much a family affair. Daughter Mary Cooper has also joined the team, in a commercial capacity. She runs the adjoining nursery, which specializes in herbaceous plants (many unusual ones), and herbs. To keep the family continuity going, her baby son is regularly seen alongside her in his pram as she tends the plants!

But it is Howard who is responsible for the extension of the garden. He has masterminded all the developments, and the two women have undertaken much of the planting up. Howard openly admits that if someone sat down and designed his 2.5-acre (1-hectare) garden on paper it would have come out quite differently. Instead, he says, he just went at it with a spade and some bits of rope to mark out the beds! It has come out remarkably well and each area, although an entity in itself, ties in with the rest of the garden.

The Front Garden

The rectangular lawns in front of the house are surrounded by borders bursting with colour over a long season. The house itself is draped with fremontodendron, roses and clematis. The area is divided from the rest of the garden by a row of spiked railings set between some charming Ham stone pillars.

The Wadi, representing a dry riverbed, is planted up with hostas, hardy geraniums and grasses.

The Wadi

The first bed beyond the railings is the Wadi, or dry riverbed border. This is an unusual idea which Howard developed on his travels abroad. In North Africa a wadi is actually a watercourse, dry except in the rainy season. The border at Lower Severalls is in reality a hollowed-out channel lined with stones and planted up on the banks with a bright array of perennial plants, in particular large clumps of hardy geraniums. A tiny bridge has been created at one end, crossing an imaginary stream. In fact this area never fills with water, and the maintenance entails little more than sweeping the stones in winter to keep them looking pristine!

The Rockery

To give what was originally a flat field a little more height, at one end of the Wadi a high rockery has been built. All the stones were hauled in from across the farm and Howard lifted each one into position by hand. He has gently sloped the stones in layers, like the seams that would be found naturally. In the soil among them a range of rockery plants are thriving. Plants that prefer shady conditions have been selected for the opposite side of the Rockery, underneath a walnut tree.

HOWARD'S ROCKERY FAVOURITES

Erigeron karvinskianus	White, tinged with pink, daisy-like flower
Thymus neiceffli	Pink flower; hairy grey needle-like leaves
Campanula portenschlagiana	Bell-shaped violet flowers; dense mat of ivy-shaped leaves

SHADE-LOVING

Dicentra 'Langtrees'	Sprays of white pendant flowers
Geranium x *cantabrigiense*	Mauvey-pink clumps
Hosta 'Francee'	Blue-green foliage, edged with white

The Pond and Bog Garden

There is no natural supply of water in the garden, so spring water from the farm has been piped in to enable the creation of a pond and an adjoining bog garden. Mary Cooper has been involved in selecting plants that will enjoy the damp conditions, and certainly some luscious growth has resulted, as she points out:

'The introduction of water means that many plants that would otherwise not do well in the garden can now be grown. To make the bog garden, a plastic liner was placed under the bed and three feet of soil piled on top. It is kept moist by the constant trickle of water piped to it.'

Bold structural plants have been used in the centre of the bed, and bright splashes of colour added around the edges, by means of heucheras and sedges.

MARY'S FAVOURITES FOR BOG GARDENS

Rheum palmatum	Rhubarb; striking long-lobed leaves, panicles of creamy flowers
Filipendula rubra 'Venusta'	Meadowsweet; tall, structural; pink flowers
Ligularia veitchiana	Large rounded leaves, yellow flower spikes
Carex elata	Tufted sedge; golden foliage with green striations
Heuchera 'Rachel'	Purple foliage, rosy pink flowers
Trollius 'Orange Princess'	Globular orange flowers, divided green leaves

The Willow Basket

Various devices are used to divide up the garden, adding interest and intrigue wherever you go. Here a hedge of roses, there a trellis strewn with honeysuckle, and every now and

Now a gardener's paradise, until a few years ago this area beyond the pillars was just farmland.

then one of Howard's ingenious home-made arches, consisting of disused pieces of agricultural equipment, such as a combine drive-shaft welded together and now overgrown with twisting climbers.

Winding paths, of just the right width for Howard on his mower – or 'mechanical Zimmer frame', as he delights in calling it – eventually lead the visitor to a curious circular hedge. This has become known as the Willow Basket. It is a living circle of willow and dogwood about 10 feet (3 metres) high and 25 feet (7.5 metres) across, with arched tubing forming the 'handle'. First a circle of coloured willow slips were planted. These quickly grew and every year Howard has carefully woven them together to create the effect of a real wicker basket. The two types of dogwood that were interplanted (*Cornus albus* 'Sibirica' and *Cornus stolonifera* 'Flaviramea') have grown so well they now dominate the willow.

Inside the basket a sheltered area has been created that is ideal for the exotic plants placed here for the summer, such as brugmansias, cannas and even a papyrus with its roots dipped into a pool of water. Over-head, meanwhile, clematis, wisteria and roses are making their way up each side of the handle, hopefully to meet eventually in the middle.

The Garden's End

Beyond the Willow Basket shrubs give way to trees. In this densely wooded area all species are native, such as ash, oak, and beech, as Howard tries to develop a wilder atmosphere that blends gradually into the surrounding countryside. The trees are closely planted, which Howard finds helps to draw them up, and later he will thin them out. The hazel will be used for coppicing.

The woodland path eventually brings you out at another pond, this time spanned by a little wooden bridge. It is a restful end to the walk, and a soothing place to sit and contemplate. Howard has brought his visitors some distance from the house by means of a range of clever designs.

He has nearly reached the boundary road, so is this the end of the line, or could he possibly want to expand further?

With a wry smile he gives his answer: 'Well, I have got the rest of the farm, but I can find plenty to do here, I think. I need to have a week when I can't find anything to do and then, well, who knows, I might take on a bit more!'

LATE SUMMER GARDENS

HADSPEN GARDEN AND NURSERY

Sandra and Nori Pope

Castle Cary, Somerset BA7 7NG

Tel. 01749 813707

LOCATION
2 miles (3 km) south-east of Castle Cary on the A371 to Wincanton.

VISITING
Open March–September, 10am–5pm, Thurs., Fri., Sat., Sun.
and Bank Holidays. Coach parties to book.

FACILITIES
Teahouse, managed by Bonds Hotel and Restaurant, near Castle Cary.
Coffee, lunch and tea served. Open April–September, 11am–5pm.
Easy access for disabled visitors; most paths hard paved.

KEY FEATURES
700-metre/yard D-shaped walled garden
Peach walk
Double yellow border
National collection of Rodgersias
Hosta collection
Colourist style

*We regard gardening as an art form. It means making pictures, by combining
certain colours. If you do find a good colour combination it takes your breath
away, and we want to create garden designs that do that for other people.*
(Sandra Pope)

It was 1987 when Nori and Sandra Pope left their nursery and the rugged scenery of their home on Vancouver Island in Canada. They set out in search of what they thought was the great colourist garden laid down by Penelope Hobhouse at Hadspen. They arrived to discover that Penelope had left nine years before and not a trace of her work around the house remained. However, what they did find was a two-acre (1-hectare) walled garden that had fallen into decay, but which exuded such a romantic and essentially English feel, the Popes were drawn to it like a magnet. Nori will never forget his first impressions:

'It was fantastic. We came on an autumn afternoon, the sun was shining and everything was gold coloured and fallen down. Blackberries grew up through the paths, and fruit was dripping from the trees. You could see the hazy outline of someone's intention of a garden. It seemed as if

The dramatic D-shaped border. A solid blanket of colour encircles the inner vegetable area.

someone had left a watercolour painting out in the rain and you could just see the outline of what was left.'

It was the vast D-shaped walled garden that impressed them above all else. In Canada there are no walled gardens, and this one was made even before Canada became a country.

So within a year the Popes had swapped their life in Canada for a new one here. It was a daring exchange, as Sandra pointed out:

'It was a huge move, but it seemed such an opportunity to come to England, this nation of gardens. If we hadn't come here we'd have missed such a big part of our garden education, because it is the Mecca of gardens and that's where we needed to be.'

The Colourist Style

It would be true to say that Sandra and Nori have an over-riding passion for colour. It is not the individual plant species that turn them on; it is their colours. The most humble plants will do, as long as they are the right shade to fit in where needed. So set are the two gardeners on achieving just the right hue that they breed for colour. They now pride themselves on having brought to life the deep mulberry red *Astrantia major* 'Hadspen Blood', along with *Papaver orientale* 'Patty's Plum', a brooding, dark wine poppy, and *Dicentra spectabilis* 'Gold Heart'.

The Popes are continuing a tradition of plant breeding at Hadspen that began earlier this century with plantsman Eric Smith, who introduced many hostas. Indeed, Nori and Sandra are making a collection of some of those original hostas in memory of his name.

It is through their use of colour that gardening at Hadspen turns into an art form:

'It's a means of making pictures, and we'll use any means to achieve our ends. If it means painting a table a different colour, to be part of the scene, then we do it. There's no limit to making the picture,' enthuses Nori.

Every working day is spent tending the plants and debating over which shades work where. With his artistic, designer background Nori is hot on why magenta works well with chartreuse, for example, and Sandra seems to have an intuitive understanding of successful combinations.

The Curved Border

This is one of the garden's most stunning features, 700 metres of solid colour in the D-shaped walled garden. It is carefully designed along the colour spectrum so that each colour merges almost imperceptibly into the next. The saturated colours of yellow, orange and red are used in the top half of the border and the half tones of pastel shades like pinks and peaches on the bottom. The border is colourful from April until September, and unlike many gardens it is especially striking in late summer.

SOME OF SANDRA'S FAVOURITE COLOUR COMBINATIONS FOR LATE SUMMER
PLUM

Clematis viticella	Mulberry plum colour, flowers until September, feathery seed-heads in winter
Cosmos atrosanguineus	Chocolate brown, smells of chocolate
Alcea rosea 'Nigra'	Hollyhock, dark mulberry
Allium sphaerocephalon	Maroon, oval-shaped
Astrantia major 'Hadspen Blood'	Blood red

PINK

Eupatorium subs. 'Purple Bush'	Purple bush, deep rose flowers
Veronica ' Pink Damask'	Pink
Geranium 'Ann Folkard'	Deep magenta pink, black eye
Cichorium intybus roseum	Ornamental chicory, 4 feet (120 cm) tall; pale pink, daisy-like flowers

The Double Yellow Border

This border, bounded on either side by tall beech hedges, keeps its colour from March until October. Early in the year pale yellows predominate, and as the quality of the light alters through the seasons, so the yellows change to become deeper and richer.

The whole concept has been painstakingly devised by Nori, who describes each yellow plant in terms of its tonality (the amount of light it absorbs), which influences its colour. The use of shades of just a single colour helps to draw the eye – and of course the body after it – through the garden. This is aided by the insertion of tall, upright plants, such as fennel, at regular intervals. Nori believes these create a beat, similar to that in music, which helps to keep the visitor moving. It is quite a different concept to that found in Monet and Jekyll gardens, which were designed for stopping and sitting in.

SOME OF NORI'S FAVOURITES FOR LATE SUMMER

Solidago 'Goldenmosa'	Goldenrod, rich, deep yellow
Foeniculum vulgare	Common fennel, feathery, yellow, upright
Rudbeckia 'Irish Eyes'	Yellow petals, green centre

Alcea rugosa	Hollyhock, pale yellow
Hakonechloa macra 'Alboaurea'	Clump-forming grass, 2 feet (60 cm) tall; chartreuse yellow

The Peach Walk

This area has a distinctly Mediterranean feel. Perched high above a rectangular lily pond, the pink and grey plants used are well suited to the sunny, south-facing, position. The name 'Peach Walk' is derived from the days when peaches were grown on the high wall that forms its backdrop. You can still see where the top of the wall has been cantilevered over to prevent peach leaf curl by keeping the rain off the leaves and fruit. It really worked! Now, however, the peaches are long gone, and the area is a mass of agapanthus, lavender, erigerons, soft cistus flowers, the tall spikes of salvias, and another Pope creation, *Anemone hupehensis* 'Hadspen Abundance'. And there still remains a large patch of the pale pink soapwort once used to make soap to clean the laundry in the big house.

MEDITERRANEAN FAVOURITES FOR LATE SUMMER

Artemisia absinthium	Silver-leaved
Erigeron karvinskianus	Blue, spiky
Cistus 'Silver Pink'	Pale pink
Agapanthus Headbourne Hybrids	Blue
Lavandula 'Sawyers'	Lavender, deep blue, silver-grey foliage
Phlomis italica	Sage-like foliage, pink flowers

The garden at Hadspen is ever-changing, and always aspiring to perfection. When you visit it you get the impression that something is brewing, that the ideas developing here are

Plants spilling from the Peach Walk into the lily pond below

on the crest of a new wave in gardening fashion. Nori and Sandra hold that strong belief too:

'What we are creating now is a style of gardening that is just beginning and will break into prominence in the twenty-first century. This is the way people will be looking at gardens.'

MIKE HASTIE

Sandra and Nori Pope

Nori's Double Yellow Border, where every plant earns its place according to its tonality

74

MARY PAYNE'S GARDEN

(Private garden)
2, Old Tarnwell, Upper Stanton Drew,
near Bristol BS39 4EA
Tel. 01275 333146

LOCATION
Directions given when appointment made by phone.

VISITING
Small groups by appointment and as advertised in
Gardens of England and Wales Open for Charity, supported by the
National Gardens Scheme ('The Yellow Book').

KEY FEATURES
Garden measures only a fiftieth of an acre (less than 100 square metres)
Front and back colour-themed

Small gardens should be coffee-time gardens. You only need to
come out with a cup of coffee and do a bit of dead-heading here and there
to keep it tidy. With intense planting there's little room for weeds.

(Mary Payne)

Mary Payne's garden proves that you don't need a large space to create a stunning effect. Her garden, bordering her small 1960s semi-detached house, covers just a fiftieth of an acre (under 100 square metres), but is packed with over 600 plant species. However, far from feeling crowded, it gives an impression of restfulness and organisation. This has been cleverly achieved, largely through the careful use of colour theming in each border. Mary is a great believer in this device in particular, because it is easier to cope with than many other design ideas, since it ties the gardener down to only certain plants and provides a structure to work around.

The Front Garden

The front garden is full of vibrant colour. Yellow is the common link in all the beds. The Bonfire Bed greets visitors as they enter the garden. It is aflame with yellows, oranges and reds, which offer a warm and cheery welcome.

'I tried to go for plants with a lot of interest,' Mary comments. 'In a small garden you can't have gaps. So plants that "perform" for a long time are very useful, for example the *Lysimachia ciliata* "Firecracker" with its dark mulberry leaves and bright yellow flowers.'

Every inch is utilized. The impressive bright red dahlia 'Bishop of Llandaff 'stands over the spot where earlier in the year Crown Imperial flowered. When one plant has finished Mary often fills the space with a plant in a pot that can be hidden amongst the foliage of the bed. To overcome the problem of terracotta drying out in summer, each pot is lined with a carrier bag which is then filled with soil. It is a successful way of retaining moisture.

Bold, strong plants that 'perform' for a long period characterize Mary's planting.

MARY'S FAVOURITES FOR A BONFIRE BED

Crocosmia 'Lucifer'	Bright, red, spiky leaves
Lysimachia ciliata 'Firecracker'	Purple foliage
Potentilla 'Gibson's Scarlet'	Red
Fuchsia magellanica 'Aurea'	Golden foliage
Ulmus minor 'Dampieri Aurea'	Golden upright elm

Further around the front garden is Mary's purple and yellow bed. 'I've used colour contrast here,' she explains, 'yellow and purple being on opposite sides of the colour wheel.'

One plant that commands and unites the whole bed is *Geranium* 'Ann Folkard'. Its startling purple flowers first show in May and continue until October. Asters add summer colour too, and the entire bed is backed by cordon fruit trees and clematis.

MARY'S FAVOURITES FOR PURPLE/YELLOW BEDS

Achillea 'Moonshine'	Grey leaves, yellow flowers
Clematis 'Polish Spirit'	Rich, dark, purple
Campanula glomerata 'Superba'	Purple bell-shaped flowers
Geranium 'Ann Folkard'	Purple flower, golden leaves
Miscanthus sinensis 'Zebrinus'	Yellow-striped grass

Finally, the yellow and white border in the front garden provides clean, crisp colours for all seasons. Evergreen shrubs and grasses are especially useful in this respect.

MARY'S FAVOURITES FOR YELLOW/WHITE BEDS

Miscanthus sinensis 'Variegatus'	Green and white grass, feathery flowers
Lamium maculatum 'White Nancy'	White-leaved variegated 'dead nettle'
Lonicera nitida 'Baggesen's Gold'	Bright green, evergreen shrub
Stipa calamagrostis	Feathery grass flowers

The Back Garden

This area is just 25 feet (7.5 metres) square. In contrast to the vibrant colours of the front, Mary has used pastel shades here because she feels they are more relaxing and conducive to sitting in the garden and enjoying it. The whole garden is enclosed by a fence with a trellis rising above it. In summer the lush growth of many clematis grow over this to give an enclosed feeling to the garden. They are pruned hard in winter to reveal the landscape behind.

In a very small space Mary has managed to work in a surprising array of features. A wooden obelisk, painted steely blue-grey, gives solidity to one corner, while in another a small stone maiden hides among the foliage beside a miniature pond. The pond is well stocked with fish and planted up with the mini water lily *Nymphaea* 'Froebelii', which will never outgrow it. A gentle trickle of water flows into the pond with the aid of a recycling pump. There is also a seat backed by a wooden rising sun (courtesy of Mary's husband) with clipped ivy growing between the rays.

A dense planting of pastel shades gives year-round cover in the back garden.

The pond, complete with mini water lilies, Nymphaea *'Froebelii', a diminutive statue and trickling waterfall.*

Mary has also managed to find a space for a small vegetable patch, screened by more trellis. Here there is just enough room for her to grow lettuces and herbs, and runner beans on a cane wigwam. In the corner stands the compost bin which enables all the greenery in the garden to be recycled.

Mary has taken into account the situation and aspect of each area, planting for sun, shade or moisture. A firm stance is adopted as far as plant choice is concerned, so as to avoid the dreaded 'dotty and messy effect', she often refers to, which she feels can easily happen in small gardens:

'I have used bold, strong, foliage. *Melianthus major*, for example, with its wonderful blue-green architectural foliage, comes up and starts to make its impact late in the season and is taking over where the astilbes and iris were earlier in the year.'

MARY'S FAVOURITES FOR A PASTEL GARDEN

Eryngium bourgatii 'Picos'	Silvery 'thistle'
Tradescantia 'Osprey'	Pale blue, fluffy stamens
Hosta 'Halcyon'	Blue
Clematis 'Comtesse de Bouchard'	Pink
Melianthus major	Blue-green architectural leaves
Rodgersia aesculifolia	Large horse chestnut-shaped leaves

For Mary, who has a family and works as a horticultural lecturer, it was essential to develop a garden that was manageable and enjoyable. By means of dense planting and year-round cover she has achieved both. Apart from a little dead-heading each week and a general tidy-up once a year, the garden generally looks after itself!

COTHAY MANOR

Alastair and Mary-Anne Robb

Greenham, near Wellington
Somerset TA21 OJR
Tel. 01823 672283

LOCATION
Turn off the A38 south of Wellington to Greenham. As you
enter Greenham turn right, signed Cothay.

VISITING
Open Wed., Thurs., Sun. 2–6pm. May–September inclusive; also
Bank Holidays. Admission: adults £3, children free.

FACILITIES
Cream teas. Small nursery. Groups welcome by appointment.
Wheelchair access.

KEY FEATURES
7-acre (3-hectare) plantsman's garden, recently restored
Garden rooms, colour-themed
200-yard/metre yew walk
Ox-bow bog garden
Specimen trees
Medieval house (open to groups by appointment)
River Tone runs through the garden

*It is a magical garden because it's so hidden. It sits in its own piece of West
Somerset which is completely unspoilt. It is very difficult to find, but you've
got to treat it as an adventure. Once you get here it is worth all the trouble.*
(Mary-Anne Robb)

Mary-Anne is not joking; the drive to Cothay can be bewildering, through a mass of tiny winding country lanes, but even these are a joy in the summer when the wild flowers are spilling from the overgrown banks. Then, when you eventually come across Cothay, it is like discovering a jewel.

The house itself has been described as the finest example of a small medieval country manor in the country. It was built in 1480 and, largely because it is so remote, has escaped the plundering that many other great houses have suffered over the generations.

The Robbs have been at Cothay for only a few years. When they arrived, although the bones of a once great garden could be seen, it had become uninteresting and overgrown. So, armed with considerable previous experience of such tasks, they set about with a will to restore this garden. They gutted the whole area, just keeping the original framework of yew hedges and garden rooms which Colonel Reginald Cooper had created in the 1930s.

Half a mile (800 metres) of yew hedging divides the many garden rooms at Cothay.

All the yew hedges surrounding the rooms have had to be severely cut back to the trunks, having become so overgrown that they almost filled the rooms they were supposed border. Even now there is so much yew hedging it takes three weeks to cut it all every September.

'We have added to the garden rooms and, just like one furnishes a house, we have furnished the garden rooms with plants and re-designed them with paths, seats and trees,' explains Mary-Anne in the bubbly effusive manner which is her trademark.

The Terrace Walk

This is an intriguing garden to visit, because there are so many different areas to explore. Entering via the grassy North Meadow, where Alastair Robb is planting many unusual trees, you suddenly discover the Terrace Walk, which runs the entire length of the house. Here after months of work ugly concrete slabs have been replaced by York stone paving and gravelled paths. The eye is drawn along the border by the repeat pattern of catmint, anthemis and gypsophila. Everywhere the tiny daisy-like flowers of *Anthemis punctata* ssp. *cupaniana* protrude from between the stones, contrasting brilliantly with the pinky-mauve *Geranium palmatum* that flowers for nearly two months in the summer.

The Green Knight's Garden

As you head back to the central lawn, the magnificent yew walk leads you into the Green Knight's Garden. Mary-Anne believes this garden room conjures up images of the days of King Arthur and his knights. Greens, silvers and whites predominate here, through the use of single white roses, climbing delphiniums and fox-tail lilies, set off by a cloud of silvery *Artemisia* 'Powis Castle'.

Emily's Garden

Passing the tinkling fountain on the parterre surrounded by neatly clipped box hedging, the next room you enter is Emily's Garden, named after the Robbs' first grandchild. Yellow is the dominant colour here. In August the *Nepeta govaniana*, *Salvia glutinosa* and *Anthemis tinctoria* turn this into a golden heaven.

The Cherry Garden

This room is shaded by a Ukon Cherry (*Prunus* 'Ukon') and is therefore filled with plants that can tolerate a lack of sun, such as hostas and ferns. The general colour scheme here is blue and white, which is taken up in the campanulas, the hardy geraniums and a clematis weaving its way through the cherry tree. An old moss-covered table, bench and bird-bath enhance the impression that here there is no hurry.

The Bishop's Room

In stark contrast to the previous colour scheme, here the bright purples and scarlets of the robes worn by bishops and cardinals are the inspiration. It is an unusual combination, but the dahlias, altstroemerias, salvias, penstemons and poppies create a rich and vibrant impression.

The ideas used in any of the individual rooms could be put into practice in even the smallest garden, which Mary-Anne believes is one of Cothay's assets: 'It is a garden for every-

Cothay, described as the finest example of a small medieval manor in the country.

body. That is its appeal. Even though it is over all a large garden, there are many small gardens within it.'

MARY-ANNE'S FAVOURITES FOR A PURPLE/SCARLET ROOM

Penstemon 'Blackbird'	Deep purple
Alstroemeria 'Marina'	Purple
Hedysarum coronarium	French honey-suckle; red
Salvia greggii 'Raspberry Royal'	Purplish red
Allium hollandicum 'Purple Sensation'	Purple; seeds through other plants

The Bog Garden

Next, wander through the herbaceous area, which creates a relaxing atmosphere among its double borders through the use of pastel colours. Then look out for the delicate alpines in

An ox-bow lake makes an ideal location for a bog garden.

This geographical feature was created when the original course of the River Tone was altered nearly seventy years ago. Even this part of the garden, however, had become a choked wilderness, and it was only after much intensive excavation that the gravel base was reached and the planting of gunneras, rodgersias and primulas could take place. Now, however, it is a charming spot where it is great fun to hop across the stepping stones with the sunlight filtering through the canopy of leaves above.

The Cottage Garden

There is always something new going on at Cothay, and the latest addition is an avenue of *Robinia pseudoacacia* 'Umbraculifera' (mop-head acacias), under-planted with catmint and summer hyacinths. Through this flowery bower you reach the little cottage garden around the back. Designed complete with cottage and picket fence, it illustrates just how simply a stunning effect can be achieved. In the drive for perfection Alastair has had all the overhead telegraph poles and cables taken down and laid underground lest they spoil the image!

The Courtyard Garden

And finally to an enclosed garden behind the church that is ablaze with the sorts of oranges, burnt siennas, and yellows that often streak across the sky in the late summer. It is another imaginative idea that is already proving a winner.

MARY-ANNE'S FAVOURITES FOR COURTYARD GARDENS

Leonotis leonurus	Orange, South African annual
Hedychium	Ginger lilies, various shades of orange;

the scree bed on the bank below. And now the bog garden appears, unusually located around an ox-bow lake.

In the Courtyard Garden the colour theme is inspired by the orange hues of the evening sky in late summer.

	need winter protection
Calceolaria biflora 'Goldcrest Amber'	Orange, rounded pouch-shaped flowers, tender
Lonicera tragophylla	Yellow honeysuckle; grows in deep shade
Rosa 'Mrs Oakley Fisher'	3 feet (1 metre) high; single, apricot rose

The resurrection of the garden at Cothay owes its success very much to teamwork. Alastair and Mary-Anne work unrelentingly, often more than twelve hours a day; in fact Mary-Anne happily describes herself as a workaholic and an obsessive. Both agree though that the restoration project has been a lot of fun, and they thoroughly enjoy showing visitors around. The Robbs are quick to point out that the team would not be complete without their trusty gardener Wesley, who often has to be persuaded to go home!

Although there are many facets to creating a successful garden, there is one strategy that Mary-Anne would highly recommend for good results:

'Continuity of planting. Always plant in groups, using odd numbers, and then have fun putting individual plants in between. This will enhance the overall effect, which may otherwise look bitty.'

AUTUMN GARDENS

WESTONBIRT ARBORETUM

Tetbury, Gloucestershire GL8 SQS
Tel. 01666 880220
Head Forester: Tony Russell
Curator: Hugh Angus

LOCATION
On the A433, 3 miles (5 km) south of Tetbury, midway
between Tetbury and the junction with the A46.

VISITING
The Arboretum grounds are open every day, 10am–8pm
(or sunset if earlier). Admission charge payable at entrance.
Groups rates for 12 or more people.

FACILITIES
Visitor centre and gift shop, plant centre and courtyard café, open daily,
10am–5pm (except Christmas and New Year). Two picnic areas (one
dog-free), next to main car parks. Toilets, including facilities for the
disabled. Limited number of wheelchairs available from visitor centre;
ring to reserve. Dog-free areas cover more than 20 per cent of the grounds.

KEY FEATURES
Walks through the acers and other trees with autumnal leaves
Night-time illuminated trail from mid-November to mid-December

*The Holford family who started the tree collection at Westonbirt had incredible
vision; they were planting trees that had never been grown in Great Britain before.
They had no idea how they were going to grow or what they would look like in
maturity. They have created, without the use of artificial follies or lakes, a unique
landscape made up of the forms, textures and foliage of the individual shrubs.*

(Tony Russell, Head Forester)

Westonbirt Arboretum is a stunning place to visit in autumn. At that time of year many of its 18,000 trees, which stretch over 600 acres (240 hectares), turn fiery colours, and its grandeur is hard to beat.

Crowds gather to admire the autumn tints in the New Acer Glade.

Nowadays the arboretum is in the hands of the Forestry Commission and it is open to anyone. This is a far cry from the days of its inception in the nineteenth century, when only the great and the good of the day were invited by the owner, Robert Holford, and later his son George, to admire the autumn hues. Over a glass of champagne, the leading Victorians of the day would vie with one another at these 'sneering parties', as they were called, each claiming they had better autumn colours in their own gardens than those at Westonbirt.

The Acer Glade

It was Robert Holford who inspired the creation of this great arboretum, now the largest in Europe. He lived in the stately Westonbirt House, (now a private girls' school) and decided he wanted to gather together one of the best collections of trees and shrubs from across the temperate world. He was to take advantage of all the newly discovered plants being brought back from across the globe by the many plant hunters of the day.

Acers became a particular favourite, and some of those originally planted can still be seen in the Old Acer Glade. It is these that hundreds of people flock to see every autumn, as Tony Russell, Head Forester, explains:

'Autumn is one of the greatest times here because of the leaves. The acers are such unique, beautiful plants. On many you can see this wonderful bonsai effect of the branches, as they twist and turn naturally, giving that very Japanese feel.'

While many of the old acers still survive, the death knell was signalled for some by the great storm of 1990. Fierce winds brought huge numbers of tall conifers crashing down onto the smaller acers below. All was not lost, though; luckily a new replacement programme was already underway.

The New Acer glade.

'In the 1960s the Forestry Commission realized the old acer glade wouldn't last for ever, so they collected seed from the original acers, propagated them and then used only the best two seedlings in every hundred to plant a new acer glade. So the new ones are even brighter than the original ones,' enthuses Tony.

An original acer in the Old Acer Glade planted by Robert Holford in the nineteenth century

He adds that at Westonbirt they can usually tell what kind of an autumn it will be by looking at the *Acer japonicum* 'Vitifolium', commonly known as the vine-leaved maple. It turns burnt reddish orange long before the other acers. If it turns early, it will be an early autumn. If it turns late, the other trees will take up their autumn tints late.

A group of miniature acers stands at the cross roads to Main Drive. They look like massive heads of henna-dyed hair, cascading down. And although they are seventy years old they stand just 5 feet (about 1.5 metres) tall.

Known as *Acer palmatum* 'Dissectum Atropurpureum', this kind of maple has delicate purple palm-like dissected leaves that grow extremely slowly and turn an eye-catching bonfire colour in autumn. Many originate from Japan, where their history is intertwined with the culture. For over two hundred years they have been grown in the Japanese temple gardens.

As with the larger acers, the trunks of these also become twisted quite naturally over time. It is this and their overall squat appearance that has made them so suitable for creating the bonsai effect, which is especially popular in Japan.

Japanese acers are particularly suitable for average-sized gardens because their total height rarely exceeds 30 feet (9–10 metres). They can tolerate most soils, although grow best on acid loams. Given dappled shade and a sheltered site, away from cold, easterly winds, especially in the spring, they should do well.

SOME OF TONY'S FAVOURITE ACERS

Acer palmatum 'Dissectum Atropurpureum'	Fiery autumn colours
Acer palmatum 'Osakazuki'	Reliably turns crimson red every autumn
Acer palmatum 'Katsura'	Apricot autumn colours
Acer palmatum 'Seiryu'	Marmalade-orange autumn colours

Westonbirt is a place of great inspiration for many, and a place where much can be learned about the important role trees play in our environment. The Head Forester here is only too aware that the place he tends and cares for is much more than just an amenity forest:

'Westonbirt is much more than a living museum. It is often described as a tree zoo. Many of the plants here are extinct in the wild, and part of our work is to propagate them and to reintroduce them into the wild. So we're doing with the trees what London Zoo is doing with pandas.'

LADY FARM

(Private garden)

Judy Pearce

Lady Farm, Chelwood, near Bristol BS18 4NN

Tel. 01761 490770

LOCATION

Take the A37 from Bristol. Turn left onto the A368 Bath road.
Lady Farm is on the outskirts of the village of Chelwood.

VISITING

By appointment and as advertised in *Gardens of England and
Wales Open for Charity*, supported by the National Gardens Scheme.
('The Yellow Book').

FACILITIES

Tea can be booked in advance. Bed and Breakfast is available;
advance booking necessary.

KEY FEATURES

6-acre (2.5-hectare) garden
All-year-round colour
Herbaceous border
Water garden
Wild-flower meadow lake
Prairie and steppe planting

*There are always titivations you can do, always plants that don't work out.
You never learn everything. I have only learnt a minimal amount in five years.
I just hope I don't run out of time, because I've got a lot more to learn.*

(Judy Pearce)

You'd never believe it, but until six years ago Judy Pearce had never done any gardening. Her farmhouse was surrounded by farm buildings where 200 dairy cows were handled and milked. When the dairy was moved, in came the diggers and bulldozed it all away.

'We were quite happy with grass five years ago, funnily enough, but after a while we got bored and developed a water feature, and it just had to have some plants around it and the garden has just grown from there,' explains Judy, who admits that gardening has now completely taken over her life!

The garden is set at the bottom of a valley where grassy fields stretch away to the horizon and beef cattle graze peacefully. The garden has developed into a series of different areas extending from the house, down the water course and

The purple and pink herbaceous border includes the purple sage, Salvia officinalis, *the maroon scabious,* Knautia macedonica, *and the pink aster,* Aster novae-angliae *'Andenken an Alma Potschke', useful repeat-flowering plants.*

around the artificial lake (complete with island and adopted swan).

The Herbaceous Border

Where once the cows collected two wide herbaceous borders now dominate the view to one side of the house. A colour theme of predominantly silvers, bronzes, purples and pinks has been chosen, and plants that give colour from March to the end of October. In contrast to many borders, in the autumn these are still a riot of flowers. Judy leaves the foliage right through the winter, so the birds and wild creatures can benefit from it (it can look especially attractive with the frost on the seed-heads), then cuts it all back in the spring.

JUDY'S FAVOURITES FOR PURPLE/PINK BORDERS IN AUTUMN

Aster novae-angliae 'Andenken an Alma Potschke'	Deep pink aster
Salvia officinalis 'Purpurascens Group'	Purple sage; good base colour
Knautia macedonica	Maroon scabious
Penstemon 'Garnet'	Ruby red
Helictotrichon sempervirens	Spiky blue grass
Miscanthus sinensis 'Kleine Fontane'	Tall grass; flowers August–winter

The Waterfall Area

The sound of gushing water draws the visitor from the herbaceous border to the head of a gentle waterfall. The large sandy-coloured rocks and the surrounding planting give the impression that this feature has been here for ever, instead of just a few years. Judy took advantage of the natural spring, and created the whole effect entirely by eye. She has quite specific views on the planting here:

In just six years this picturesque setting has been developed from a field.

Yellow Rudbeckia fulgida *var.* deamii *and the striking green leaves of* Cornus alba *'Aurea' frame the water course which runs down the valley.*

'The plants we have chosen here associate well with water, such as the little water forget-me-not, which is marvellous for softening the edges. I like to plant in large, bold blocks, with lots of the same kind of plant in each area to give the most stunning effect, as I have done with the golden cornus and the brilliant yellow rudbeckias.'

JUDY'S FAVOURITES FOR WATERSIDES IN AUTUMN

Rudbeckia fulgida var. *deamii*	Golden cone flower
Cornus alba 'Aurea'	Golden/green leaves; red stems in winter

The Wild-flower Meadow

Even in autumn the seedy heads of the grasses look attractive swaying in the breeze, with the bright faces of the ox-eye daisies gleaming against the late sun. To create this effect Judy sprayed off the original rye grass and replanted with a mixture of ten different grasses, to which were added some ox-eye daisy seed. The meadow was under-sown with hundreds of the tiny purple *Allium sphaerocephalon* to give some summer colour.

The Prairie

Rounding a corner at the top of the hill, a whole new look greets the unsuspecting visitor. On what was a steep, stony, problem area, Judy has introduced a scheme using the prairie planting method that has become so popular, especially in the United States and Germany. It was suggested by her friend and adviser, Mary Payne (whose garden is featured on pages 75–8). Judy describes the effect:

'It is a mixture of 15 per cent grasses with herbaceous hardy perennials. They are all densely planted in drifts, providing lots of autumn colour. I have tried to continue the yellow and orangey colour theme with the flowers, in particular the *heleniums*. The idea is that it is very low maintenance. It is all covered with bark mulch, and the only work required is to strim it all down in February, rake it off and it should all grow back again!'

JUDY'S PRAIRIE FAVOURITES

Helenium autumnale 'Moerheim Beauty'	Rusty colour
Artemisia ludoviciana 'Silver Queen'	Silvery
Euphorbias	Various greens
Miscanthus sinensis 'Zebrinus'	Striped grass
Calamagrostis x *acutiflora* 'Karl Foerster'	Grass/vertical flower spikes
Liatris spicata	Purple/white flower spikes

*Grasses and herbaceaous hardy perennials work well in
the low-maintenance prairie planting scheme.*

Rudbeckiaf ulgida var. *sullivantii* 'Goldsturm'	Golden; late-flowering

The Steppe Area

In contrast to the thickly planted, bark-mulched prairie, further on down the slope the steppe area is more sparsely planted, with lower-growing species that thrive in drier conditions. It is mulched with stone. This idea originates from the great steppes of Russia, where white and silver plants and many grasses stand up well to the inhospitable climate.

From Judy's point of view, this area is low maintenance and provides cover and colour for most of the year. It still looks good in autumn, with delicate annual poppies blazing in groups of yellow and orange, the grasses softly blowing in the wind and the last few bees still buzzing around the deep purple oreganum. Although only in its first season it is already a winner with Judy:

'If anyone were to ask me which was my favourite part of the garden, I would have to say it's this,' she says. 'I never thought I would say this, but I love it to bits.'

JUDY'S FAVOURITES FOR STEPPE AREAS

Pennisetum villosum	Low-growing, feathery grass
Stipa tenuissima	Fine, flowing grass
Origanum laevigatum 'Herrenhausen'	Deep purple flower; bee attractant
Euphorbia polychroma	Greeny yellow foliage
Coreopsis verticillata	Yellow daisy-like plant; long-flowering, fine-leaved
Eschscholzia californica	Bright yellow/orange /red annual poppies

Judy Pearce is an inspiration to anyone who is just starting out on the gardening trail. Her garden shows what is possible within just a short space of time, even if you are beginning with no knowledge at all. Now her garden has become her all-consuming passion.

'I don't regret it for a minute,' she comments. 'It is a real haven down here, and I could easily become quite a little hermit.'

PRIOR PARK LANDSCAPE GARDEN

Church Lane, Widcombe, Bath BA2 6BD.

Tel. 01225 833422
Head Gardener: Matthew Ward

LOCATION

No car park, so travelling by bus, or on foot, is advisable. Badgerline buses nos. 2 and 4 to Prior Park main gates depart from Bath city centre bus station (by Dorchester Street) every ten minutes from 9.45am, Mon.–Sat.; Sun. and Bank Holidays, every half hour.

VISITING

Open from noon to 5.30pm (or dusk, if earlier), 6 days a week, except Tues. Closed Christmas Day, Boxing Day and New Year's Day. Admission charge: £3.80 adults, £1.90 children (£1 discount if public transport used). National Trust members free (plus £1 voucher for using public transport).

FACILITIES

Toilets. Three spaces for disabled drivers (must be booked in advance). Wheelchair access to top of garden only.

KEY FEATURES

Eighteenth-century landscape garden
Spectacular views over Bath
1-mile (1.6-km) circular walk

The highly significant thing about this garden it that while Ralph Allen was creating it, between 1734 and 1764, the English landscape style developed, and that is our most important contribution to the history of art in the world.
(John Sales, Head of Gardens, National Trust)

Prior Park Landscape Garden offers splendid vantage points from which to view the city of Bath.

Since the garden is too small and too steep to fit in a car park without siting it over an archaeological site, visitors are encouraged to get to Prior Park by means of public transport. And indeed it couldn't be easier, for buses regularly leave the city centre bus station and climb the steep drive to the main gate.

Once you arrive, be prepared for a bracing walk, since the mile-long (1.6-km) route is fairly steep in parts! However, the breathtaking views that greet you make it all extremely worth while. (If the walk seems too much, just sit at the top and admire the spectacle before you!)

It is really the dramatic site which makes this garden. It is located in a steep-sided valley running down to the famous Palladian Bridge at the bottom and looking over the City of Bath. At the head of the valley is the imposing Prior Park mansion, built by the man who was the inspiration behind the whole creation, Ralph Allen. (It is now a private school.)

Ralph Allen was an entrepreneur and philanthropist, and he chose this site because he was trying to sell Bath stone, and he built his house to advertise it. From its imposing location it could be seen and admired by all of the city. The advertisement obviously worked, for Mr Allen's stone was used to turn Bath into a splendid Palladian attraction.

Ralph Allen, who made his first fortune by reorganizing the postal system, developed the garden from the mid-eighteenth century until his death in 1764. During this time he continuously landscaped, planted and gardened it in three distinct phases. And although the 28-acre (11.3-hectare) landscape fell into decay later, remarkably it has survived virtually unchanged.

The English Landscape Style

The garden is regarded as being of the archetypal eighteenth-century English Landscape Style, about which John Sales, garden historian for the National Trust, is most enthusiastic:

'It was an attempt to create an idealized impression of nature based on a classical landscape. Many of the wealthy of the day went on grand tours of Europe and when they returned they wanted to re-create what they had seen. It is not a natural landscape but many people now look on it as such.'

Allen was heavily influenced in his design ideas by two great men of the time: the poet Alexander Pope and, later, the landscape designer Capability Brown. Pope was a pioneer of the landscape movement. It was he who moved away from the formal design initially laid out at Prior Park and encouraged Allen to develop the wilderness on the west side. This included a grotto, a serpentine lake and a sham bridge. These are the first areas you pass on the circular walk, before even seeing the mansion and the views across Bath.

'It was Capability Brown who later swept away the cascade and pond that had been in the centre of the valley and graded the valley into a flowing landscape that united all the parts, giving the impression of an idealized natural landscape,' explains John Sales.

The Palladian Bridge

From the mansion, the eye cannot fail to be attracted by the Palladian Bridge located over a lake at the bottom of the valley. The path leads down to it, and even from a distance its classical style is obvious. It was only the third such structure to be built in England, after those at Wilton and Stowe. It was based on an Italian bridge that was roofed to keep out the snow. Allen had his made by Richard Jones in 1755.

The bridge stands on the first of three dams which form a cascade through the central arch. As well as being seen as a

The newly restored Palladian Bridge.

Graffiti dating from the eighteenth century adorn the pillars on the Palladian Bridge.

eighteenth century, such as yew, euonymous, ferns, philadelphus and viburnum.

The Sham Bridge, designed to look like a bridge over a river as one approached, has also been restored and looks resplendent once again. (There is of course no river; it is a clever piece of trickery!)

The Palladian Bridge, based on an Italian design, was roofed to keep out the snow.

bridge over apparently continuous water, it was framed by hanging woods. It had fallen into a sad state of disrepair when the National Trust took over the garden in 1995, and they have spent £400,000 on its restoration. Even the eighteenth-century graffiti etched into the stone pillars have been preserved!

Restoration

Head Gardener Matthew Ward has been masterminding a massive clearance and restoration programme. Years of undergrowth had to be hacked through in order to lay paths that would enable visitors to get round. Much thinning is still continuing within the woods that frame the valley. And while there are no exact planting plans to follow in the restoration work, replanting schemes are being put into operation using plants that would have been available in the

The Sham Bridge

Matthew has many more plans for Prior Park Landscape Garden, which include resurrecting the Serpentine Lake leading to the Sham Bridge and reinstating the rocky cascade that should crash down into the Wilderness Area.

Apart from the unique place it has in the history of gardening in this country, it is the unexpected discovery of the garden, hidden in its sheer valley so close to the city, that makes it special.

It caught one recent visitor quite by surprise: 'It is absolutely beautiful,' they exclaimed. 'I would recommend it to anyone. I only live around the corner and I had no idea it was here.'

There is, however, an element of uncertainty hanging over the garden. Planning permission to open was granted only in 1998. Renewal of permission hinges on the success of the Green transport scheme delivering visitors to the garden. So if you want to ensure this wonderful attraction is preserved for ever, and that future generations can benefit from seeing it, make sure you go to the Landscape Garden by bus!

WINTER GARDENS

STOURHEAD

Stourton, Warminster
Wiltshire BA12 6QD
Tel. 01747 841152
Head Gardener: Richard Higgs

LOCATION

Stourhead is located in the village of Stourton, signed from the A303,
5 miles (8 km) north of Mere.

VISITING

The garden is open daily, 9am–7pm (or sunset if earlier). Admission
£4.40 adults, £2.40 children. House open Easter–end October.
Admission: adults £4.40, children £2.40; combined admission
to house and garden: £7.90 adults, £3.70 children.
Free to National Trust members. Tours by appointment.

FACILITIES

Tearoom, shop, pub serving hot food in the garden.

KEY FEATURES

Eighteenth-century landscape garden with extensive
collection of trees and shrubs.

*The garden is a work of art. Henry Hoare was innovative and daring, and
Stourhead was very much a new thing and a new style. Henry was showing
that he was leading the latest fashion, known as the English Landscape Style.*
(Richard Higgs, Head Gardener)

Even at the massive stone archway at the entrance to Stourhead House, you know you are heading for something grand. The driveway lined with the huge gnarled trunks of ancient sweet chestnut trees curves round to reveal the splendid Palladian mansion at the top. This was where Henry Hoare II came to live in 1741, at the age of thirty-six, and where, just a few years later, he was inspired to create a garden that is now regarded as a work of art and as the epitome of the eighteenth-century English landscape movement.

Henry Hoare became known to his family as 'the Magnificent', which suggests the lifestyle and ambition which made Stourhead. He succeeded to the family banking business on his father's death and it was this that funded his gardening projects. The Hoare connection with the bank still continues today, although Stourhead passed into the hands of the National Trust in 1946.

Extensive lawns and views over the ha-ha to the surrounding countryside dominate around the house. The real garden tour begins well away from the house, however, in the valley below, where Henry Hoare took advantage of the natural features to create his masterpiece. Here three valleys converged with the springs of the River Stour running through them, and the soil was good. So with the help of one professional architect the landscape gardens of

Stourhead House

Stourhead were developed. They became an English invention that contrasted sharply with the formal avenues, canals, parterres and artificial effects so admired in Europe in the early eighteenth century.

'Although Stourhead is famed for the blaze of colour provided by the daffodils and rhododendrons later in the year, for garden purists, winter is actually the best time to come to Stourhead. It is at this time that its structure can best be seen,' enthuses Head Gardener Richard Higgs.

Henry 'the Magnificent' intended visitors to get the maximum anticipation and surprise from his garden, and to do this even today they should enter via the Fir Walk, beyond the house. From here the circuit takes an hour and a half to two hours, although those less inclined or able can simply take in the views from the village end of the lake, rather than following the whole route.

The Temple of Apollo

'The garden is really a series of glimpses and views that unfold as you go round,' explains Richard Higgs. The first glimpse seen from the path that snakes around the whole valley is of the Temple of Apollo. This then becomes a focal point, drawing visitors on around the garden, eventually to finish the walk high up beside the temple. Round, with a

The Pantheon

domed roof and Corinthian columns, it was designed by Henry Flitcroft and built in 1765.

The route around the garden is circuitous, so that all the treats in store are not revealed at once. In devising the layout, Henry Hoare was much influenced by the eighteenth century quotation 'For what is more tedious than for the foot to travel where the eye has gone before?'

The Pantheon

The next view across the lake through the woods is of the elegant Pantheon, another of Henry Flitcroft's designs, and the most important temple at Stourhead. It serves as a focus for the whole scene, giving it its classical character, and reflecting the original Pantheon built by the Romans.

'Henry Hoare would have done the grand tour of Italy like many wealthy men of his day, and the classical images he saw obviously influenced his plans for the garden back here in Wiltshire,' the Head Gardener expounds as he strides around this great garden, of which he never tires.

With its fine columns and domed rotunda, the Pantheon was intended to house Rysbrack's statue of Hercules and many other sculptures evoking the heyday of ancient Rome. The Pantheon was originally heated, which suggests it was used for entertainment by Henry and his friends down by the lake – a grand place from which to show off the garden! Views from here across the glistening lake to the church and village of Stourton are stunning.

The Grotto

About halfway around the lake a path diverts down some winding moss-lined steps into a dank grotto below. Grottos were typical of the eighteenth century; every great garden had to have one. At Stourhead the clear spring waters of the River Stour proved ideal for the creation of the underground pools. Here statues of the River God and the Nymph of the Grot have amused visitors for centuries. An 'Ode to the Nymph' by Alexander Pope, that great exponent of the landscape movement, can still be clearly defined etched into the white marble beside her pool. The cave is cleverly built from eroded, water-washed limestone and even from here there is a view out across the lake.

From the Grotto the path wends its way past the Pantheon, which looks even more impressive from close quarters. Next, as you cross the dam which holds in the water for the lake, a gushing waterfall attracts your attention away to the right. It was designed by one of Henry Hoare's friends, Copplestone Warre Bampfylde, who was responsible for a landscape garden at Hestercombe House, near Taunton.

Richard Higgs, Head Gardener at Stourhead

At last, after a steep climb the Temple of Apollo, first seen from the other side of the valley, is gained. The panoramas that open up from here are breathtaking. From this vantage point the entire scene can be taken in, as the garden's creator intended.

After Henry the Magnificent

Successive owners of Stourhead continued to develop it, mainly through the planting. Sir Richard Colt Hoare, who inherited Stourhead in 1785, introduced rhododendrons and many of the newly imported cedars, Douglas firs and exotics. Many more flowering shrubs and rhododendrons were planted later by Sir Henry Hoare in the early twentieth century.

The plant collection at Stourhead is now regarded as one of the most important woody plant collections in Britain. It is renowned for its high proportion of conifers, many from China, Japan, North America and the Himalayas. A stately *Pinus peuce* (Macedonian pine), is one of the original introductions still surviving in the garden. It came from the South West Balkans in 1845. Another original tree is a massive *Thuja plicata* (Western red cedar) which is 140 years old and has extended itself so enormously by layering that you can now walk right through it!

In 1946 the Hoare family, forced by taxation pressures, handed over Stourhead to the safekeeping of the National Trust. The current Henry Hoare has vivid memories of the garden when the family still owned it:

'I first came to live here when I was sixteen, but had often played here before that as a young child. In those days it was very overgrown, there were masses of rhododendrons and you could hardly see the lake, so the National Trust have opened it up considerably. They have done an excellent job

The Macedonian pine, Pinus peuce, *is one of the original introductions to the garden that still survives.*

and not without problems, for it was designed only for occasional small numbers of visitors, but now there are thousands and it is rather a different concept.'

However, for the tenth Henry Hoare, handing over such

a family heirloom has not been without its sad moments:
    'There has always been a tinge of regret, but I still have a great sense of pride that the man who created all this was a member of my family. Indeed we're still very proud of the fact that we have also retained the family banking business that first made the money that was used to fund Stourhead.'

RICHARD'S FAVOURITE STOURHEAD TREES

Richard Higgs has some particular favourites among the trees in the collection, many of which would be choice specimens for the amateur gardener.

Picea smithiana	West Himalayan spruce; large conifer with distinct drooping branches and long, dark green needles
Fraxinus ornus	Manna ash; medium-sized tree; flowers in May; attractive smooth bark
Hamamelis mollis	Chinese witch hazel; large shrub/small tree; sweetly scented golden yellow flowers December–March; good autumn colour
Abies procera	Noble fir; large tree of rounded habit; bluish-green needles and magnificent cones; masses of yellow flowers in March before leaves
Acer opalus	Italian maple; medium-sized tree of rounded habit; masses of yellow flowers in March before leaves

STICKY WICKET

(Private garden)

Pam and Pete Lewis

Buckland Newton, Dorchester, Dorset DT2 7BY

Tel. 01300 345476

LOCATION

In Buckland Newton, 11 miles (18 km) from Dorchester and Sherborne;
2 miles (3 km) east of A352 or take the B3143 from Sturminster Newton.
The garden is located at the T-junction midway the church, school and
'Gaggle of Geese' pub.

VISITING

Thurs., June–September, 10.30am–8pm. Various weekend dates in June and
August as outlined in *Gardens of England and Wales Open for Charity*
('The Yellow Book'). Admission: £2.50. adults, children £1.

FACILITIES

Free parking. Wheelchair access. Guide dogs only. Teas available. Parties
by appointment. Good pub lunches at nearby 'Gaggle of Geese' pub.

KEY FEATURES

2-acre (1-hectare) artistically designed wildlife garden
Frog garden, bird garden, white garden and round garden
Wild-flower meadow, sheep fold
Willow sculptures

*As ex-farmers we had watched what had happened to the countryside, and we
thought we'd like to do a bit to redress the balance. So we set out deliberately to
develop an eco-haven. And since I am interested in garden design and plant
associations I saw no reason why the various ideas shouldn't be combined.*

(Pam Lewis)

Sticky Wicket is an unusual and memorable name for a garden. It was so called by the previous owners, who were addicted to cricket despite the unsuitable heavy, clay soil. Pam and Peter Lewis took over the place in 1986. It was badly in need of draining, and the surrounding pastures had become sadly neglected.

With a shared interest in wildlife and conservation, the couple wanted to create a garden that would connect with their smallholding and unfold imperceptibly into the beautiful Dorset countryside surrounding them. Pam was already working in the garden design field and, after carefully researching the plants that would be most beneficial to wildlife as well as visually pleasing, she set about creating her own garden plan.

While the garden is open to visitors only in summer and autumn, it still manages to look attractive at all times of the year.

One of Sticky Wicket's regular visitors

Everything Pam does is with the wildlife in mind:

'We have selected plants that provide for the wildlife throughout the year, supplying pollen, nectar, fruits and seeds. The way the garden is managed is also crucial. It is important not to cut down too much material in the autumn, for this will provide protection and food for the birds. Areas that are going to be used as their nesting sites should be pruned early.'

When we filmed at Sticky Wicket, it was mid-winter, and there was a thick blanket of snow on the ground. It was a magical time to visit. The crisp snow was hanging heavy on the seed-heads, and the bright berries were brilliant against the white background. At every turn some artistic creation was placed to catch the eye. And as if to prove that their wildlife methods were working, the whole place was teeming with wild birds eager for the feast of food provided for them.

'The design of the garden radiates from the house,' Pam told us. 'All paths from the house lead to the parts of the garden we visit the most. Each of the four main gardens has a different style, atmosphere and focus which is reflected in the planting associations. And each has an individual colour scheme.'

The Frog Garden

'Every wildlife garden should have a pond for frogs, toads and dragonfly larvae,' says Pam. The area is themed in tones of yellow and blue for spring and summer, and all species are native. In winter a dramatic effect is created by spectacularly coloured cornus stems.

PAM'S FAVOURITES FOR A FROG GARDEN

Cornus alba 'Elegantissima'	Maroon stems in winter
Cornus alba 'Kesselringii'	Dark maroon stems in winter
Rodgersia podophylla	Bold architectural leaves, textured white flowers and bronze young foliage
Deschampsia cespitosa 'Goldschlier'	Airy straw-coloured grass; long-lasting
Hosta 'Honey Bells'	Limey-green hosta

The bird theatre. Rows of hand-crafted bird feeders hang outside the kitchen window.

The Bird Garden

'This is our theatre in the winter. We have gone to a lot of trouble to bring the focus of attention close to the house at this time of year,' Peter tells us as he fills up the countless bird feeders for the second time that morning.

Even the feeders are attractive. Pam has decorated them with woven willow and cut out faces in coconut shells. They hang in a line from the pergola in front of the kitchen window, giving Pam and Pete a close up view of all the activity. Over sixty species of bird are attracted to the garden, including spotted woodpeckers (who enjoy the fat poles), nuthatches and siskins, as well as dozens of blue tits and greenfinches. Even a fox slopes in, and tucked away in specially made boxes lacewings and ladybirds hibernate. The sides of the house are also adorned with nesting boxes.

It is at this time of year that the Lewises know they are getting the mix right for wildlife; the sheer numbers visiting their garden tell the story.

PAM'S FAVOURITES FOR THE BIRDS IN WINTER

Cotoneaster x watereri 'John Waterer'	Brilliant red berries, lasting longer than other species
Berberis thunbergii 'Atropurpurea Nana'	Low-growing; black berries complement the foliage
Geranium sanguineum var. *striatum*	Long-flowering, low-growing; mid-pink, colouring up in autumn; seeds in winter
Rosa eglanteria	Sweet briar; apple-scented, thorny plant for nesting; copious rose hips
Mahonia japonica	Winter flowering; summer berries; good cover

The Round Garden

The flowing colours of nectar-rich flowers in the maze-like Round Garden are best seen between May and October. However, on frosty winter days the seed-heads can still look magnificent. Little is cleared here until the spring, to provide food and cover for the wild creatures.

PAM'S FAVOURITE SEED PLANTS FOR WINTER

Lythrum salicaria	Purple loosestrife; good stems and seed-heads
Perovskia atriplicifolia 'Blue Spire'	White blooms on vertical spires of stems; good cover

Sedum spectabile	Burnt sienna-coloured flowers, flat heads, and good winter seeds
Monarda 'Blue Stocking'	Bergamot; round, long-lasting seed-heads
Allium sphaerocephalon	Oval silvery seed-heads

The Sheep Fold

When you venture up to the top of the garden, past the pen full of domestic wildfowl and the dovecote with its cooing white doves, you will find an old shepherd's caravan. Pam and Peter use this as a hide from which to study the wildlife.

Beside the caravan Pam has been busy weaving a willow witch out of coppiced material from elsewhere in the garden. It is an activity Pam loves to get involved in during the winter. Not only does it mean that she can develop quirky artistic features to entertain visitors later on, it also helps with recycling in the garden. In fact, all the hedge-cutting and pruning materials are reused, whether it be for sculpture, fencing, arbours, firewood or simply feeding the goats!

Indoors

Even the Christmas decorations at Sticky Wicket are out of the ordinary. They are all made from coloured stems or interesting pieces of branches hung with fairy lights or woven to hold candles. Pam has also designed a 'Magic Tree' from a branch of contorted hazel. It is decked with little gifts of nuts, berries and lard balls for the birds, as well as other small children's presents. When all the treasures are gone, the branch can simply be stuck into the ground and it should take root!

A willow witch woven by Pam Lewis, one of the many artistic features that adorn the garden

PAM'S FAVOURITES FOR ARTISTIC CREATIONS

Salix alba vitellina 'Britzensis'	Willow; red stems with yellow underside, look good embedded in terracotta pots
Corylus avellana 'Contorta'	Contorted hazel; highly twisted
Salix babylonica 'Tortuosa'	Contorted willow, ashen colour

Pam and Peter open their garden to the public in the hope that they may inspire other gardeners to do something for wildlife, to help combat the habitat destruction that is going on everywhere. Although it can only be on a small scale, Pam is convinced that every little helps.

As she told us: 'Ten years on from the beginning of the growth of our garden Pete and I look at it and feel very satisfied with what we have done. Sometimes we are actually quite in awe of the results we have had, particularly with the wildlife, and especially the huge increase in the bird population. The general balance has got to the point where we don't have to use any pesticides or fungicides even if we wanted to.'

PARNHAM HOUSE AND GARDENS

John and Jennie Makepeace

Beaminster, Dorset DT8 3NA. Tel. 01308 862204

LOCATION
From Crewkerne take the A356 Dorchester road and turn right onto
the A3066 to Bridport. Parnham is approximately half a mile
(800 metres) out of Beaminster on the Bridport road.

VISITING
Open April–October, Sun., Tues., Wed., Thurs. and Bank Holidays,
10am–5pm. Admission: adults £5, children £2. Parties by appointment.

FACILITIES
Licensed restaurant.

KEY FEATURES
Topiary
Sculptures
Herbaceous borders
Play area, willow tunnel and playhouse
Restored sixteenth-century manor house, exhibiting
twentieth-century furniture made by John Makepeace

*I am my own head gardener, and I do find it an enormous challenge having
a garden that is constantly on show. In effect one is gardening for other people,
and in an historic garden which is associated with a Grade I listed house it
really is quite a responsibility.*

(Jennie Makepeace)

arnham exudes creative spirit. It is from the house that furniture designer and master craftsman John Makepeace produces his works of art and runs a school of design and craftsmanship, and the sixteenth-century manor house provides an ideal display area for the twentieth-century pieces of furniture made here.

Jennie Makepeace has her own artistic skills, and they shine through in the 14-acre (5.5-hectare) gardens that surround and complement the house. For twenty years she has painstakingly been restoring the gardens to the state they were in when created in 1911. She has also added many of her own new designs, as she explains:

'When we first came here there had been a skeleton staff who had not planted anything for nearly twenty-five years. So everything you see that is not big, I planted, which includes the herbaceous borders, the Portuguese laurels, and the rose beds. It has been a massive task and is still on-going; it is never finished.'

With just a small staff to help her now, Jennie is usually to be seen somewhere in the garden, planting,

Jennie Makepeace

weeding or pruning. During breaks between filming she managed to prune the whole of a giant wisteria growing along the terrace wall!

A walk around the gardens will take you through a large variety of different areas, from the structured and formal to the gentler herbaceous borders and even into a wooded area beside the rushing River Brit.

The Ladies' Terrace

This is the first of three terraces, and runs beside the house at the top level. The layout is one of gravel paths and neatly mown lawns spawning exotic lollipop-shaped Portuguese laurel trees. These are often mistaken for bay trees, but are much more uncommon. The idea was all Jennie's, and over eight years she has carefully coaxed them into this shape using a hooped template to clip around.

Unusual shapes predominate elsewhere on this terrace in the form of some giant yew topiary, one like a massive tractor-wheel turned on its side, the other a snaking spiral.

The Yew Terrace

From the edge of the Ladies' Terrace you are met with a majestic vista down over the Yew Terrace below. Two massive squares are perfectly marked by fifty conical yews, each precisely clipped to the same shape. These were the inspiration of the unknown garden designer in 1911, for whom Jennie has great admiration:

'Whoever planted these must have had great foresight,' she remarks. 'We are still researching who could have designed it. It may just have been a brilliant amateur.'

Jennie herself has worked hard to return the yews, which had become sadly misshapen, to their former glory and to replace dead specimens with new ones. She and her team have devised another cunning template that rotates around the tree to aid clipping. It takes about three weeks to clip all

Portuguese laurels, Prunus lusitanica *'Myrtifolia', grace the Ladies' Terrace at Parnham.*

the yews and the cuttings are in great demand for cancer research.

The two yew squares are divided by a central path, beside which rushes water from a natural gravity-fed stream in two rills. And from everywhere the soft honey-coloured stonework of the house and the framework of the garden forms a backdrop. In fact the entire garden is remarkably strong on structure:

Some of the fifty conical yews on the Yew Terrace

'Well, I think structure is the basis of a good garden. Once you have got the bones right you can have fun with flowers later,' explains Jennie. 'The house, originally built in 1540, had major restoration work done in 1810 by John Nash, who built Buckingham Palace. Then along comes someone else a hundred years later and does this wonderful balustrade and the gazebos in the garden in the very same mode of thought. It is a wonderful combination!'

Yew topiary is a special feature of the garden.

The Parkland and Lake

The whole garden is set in eighteenth-century parkland, where many of the original trees still survive. The garden ends at a lake, which has been reinstated and restocked with fish.

Jennie is pleased with the development: 'It's a nice punctuation mark, and much better than the wilderness we found here when we arrived.'

The Courtyard Garden

This is the latest addition to the gardens. It was built three years ago following a design by Paul Cooper, a gold-medal winner at Chelsea Flower Show. The focal point is a sculpture by John Maine in smooth Portland stone. The hard landscape of flagstones, cobbles and gravel is softened by grey and silver plants.

Just opposite the courtyard is a play area, delightfully equipped with a willow wigwam with a tunnel and a willow tree house, situated above a pets' graveyard, which will intrigue children.

Wandering further afield through the herbaceous borders that line the old herringbone-brick path, you come to a woodland walk and a final surprise: Nick Munro's giant electric-blue sculpture of the two comedians Morecambe and Wise. They appear somewhat absurd standing among the trees, but it all adds to the spice of Parnham!

JENNIE'S FAVOURITE PLANTS FOR STRUCTURE

Prunus lusitanica 'Myrtifolia'	Portuguese laurel; evergreen; can be trained and clipped into shape
Rhamnus alaternus 'Argenteovariegata'	Italian buckthorn; evergreen, variegated; can be clipped into shape against a wall
Phormium tenax	New Zealand flax; evergreen, spiky; various colours, including bronze, green and yellow
Buxus sempervirens	Box; fast-growing; good for topiary
Taxus baccata 'Fastigiata'	Irish yew; erect, columnar habit

The House

No visit is complete without venturing inside the house to see the furniture designed by John Makepeace. As with Munro's sculpture, many may find the juxtaposition of the modern in the extremely old setting somewhat unexpected, but this is just what Makepeace wanted, as he explains:

119

Furniture designed by John Makepeace is exhibited in Parnham House.

throughout history the most exciting things are the most progressive.'

Wood is the basis for all the furniture, and at the heart of Makepeace's inspiration:

'Wood will make a contribution to all the things we want if we want a sustainable future. So managing our woods using forest produce is central to our survival.'

And that is why the very location of Parnham, surrounded by woodlands, is so fitting. Sometimes, however, much as Jennie loves the place, its pressures need to be left behind. So she has had her own little house of straw made, tucked away from it all, where she can escape to contemplate.

'I love the combination of old with new. People think that they live in an old house, so they must have old furniture, but design is something continuous, it goes on, and always

'I do think everyone needs a room of their own,' she says, 'especially women. Even if it is only at the bottom of the garden.'